When Heaven Speaks

ARE YOU LISTENING?

Copyright ©2022 by Kimberly Washington

All rights reserved.

ISBN 978-0-578-29155-0

Devotions for Every Week of the Year

KIMBERLY WASHINGTON

When Heaven Speaks

PRESENTED TO
_____

FROM
_____

DATE
_____

Special Note: _____
_____
_____
_____
_____
_____
_____
_____

Many Thanks

These individuals have encouraged, critiqued, applauded, and uplifted me during this process. They helped to bring this assignment to fruition with their continued love and support. To each of them, I offer my most sincere gratitude and appreciation.

Alice M. Baker – the great encourager. You said to me, "Who do you think you are to tell God no," when He first presented this assignment to me. I didn't think I was equipped or good enough to write such a devotional or anything, for that matter, but you reminded me that if God brought me to it, He will, without a doubt, get me through it. You reminded me that I am enough. When I wanted to run from the process, you told me I had to stay, fight, and endure to get to where God wanted to take me. Thank you for not letting me quit and for keeping me accountable to the process of breaking free from my CZ (comfort zone).

Debbie Hollingsworth – my other mother. You have always been there when I needed a shoulder to cry on or a listening ear when I needed to vent. You are one of the most kitchen-savvy people I know. Thank you for letting me read to you what I have written and for liking it.

Krystal Robinson – the brave one. It has been a very rough ride at times, but you have never given up hope. No sickness can keep you down. You are a perfect example of what God can do if only we would trust Him. Thank you for being a good big sister and for showing me and the world what real perseverance and faith in God looks like.

Gail Smith — the skillful one. When I think of you, I think of someone who is gifted. You are so skillful at so many things, and you don't hoard your knowledge. You sing! You are a musician like none other. Your administrative abilities are second to none and you are always willing to share what you know. Thank you for providing great editing for this assignment. Thank you for stepping in and up after Mother was gone. You've been a really good big sister through the years, and I so appreciate who you are and all you do.

Dr. Kim Monette — my dear friend. When life got hard and scary, you were my hand up. You were one of the first two people who knew I was writing this devotional and kept my secret. Thank you for being one of my biggest supporters and believing in my ability to deliver a good message.

Tize Williams — my Tize! You are so incredibly talented. Thank you for always being your wonderful, creative, and authentic self. God blessed you with the gift of the spoken word, and I pray that it will always make room for you. Thank you for so willingly accepting my request. You really outdid yourself. May your desires always align with His will for your life, and may you be granted the desires of your heart.

Min. Debra D. Jones — the worldwide barrier breaker. You are truly a gem—an example for so many women. Thank you for providing a platform for us to venture out on our journey of discovery. Thank you for helping so many to realize that not only do we have gems on the inside of us but that we, too, are gems—often hidden, in plain sight, behind our fears, our past failures, and rejections. Thank you for helping us to be brave and "faith-it" past our apprehensions.

My Family — my foundation. I'm so grateful for my upbringing—one where love was instilled in us at a young age. We may not always agree on everything, but we do not fuss or fight and hold grudges against one another. Thank you for putting up with me all these years. Whenever I have needed any of my siblings, you all have always been there for me. I have never gone under, and never will, because of you. For all of my nieces and nephews, my favorite cousins (you're all my favorite but don't tell Ronnie), and aunts and uncles who have loved, prayed, and cared for me, thank you from the bottom of my heart. You all are the funniest people I know. So thankful for all the laughs and the joy you have brought to my life.

God – my good, good Heavenly Father. Lord, you have been better than good to me and my loved ones down through the years. I am so humbled that you have entrusted me with such a grand assignment. It is my prayer that you are pleased with the outcome. I am forever grateful that you have given me purpose in writing this devotional and have so mercifully permitted me to walk out that purpose with You. When I did not feel like I had much to offer, you gave me not only purpose but an amazing assignment. Thank you for seeing me and calling me by name. It is truly in You that I live, breathe, and have my being. Help me to always present my body as a living sacrifice, holy and acceptable. This is my reasonable service to You.

For Mother

The Reasons Why

As the story goes, at my birth, my parents were given an ultimatum; save the child or the mother, but it certainly couldn't be both. You see, I was premature, and things weren't looking too good for the home team. So, the prayer warriors gathered, and it was declared in the heavens that neither one of us would die but live out the days God had promised. Now, forty-nine years later, here I sit, putting pen to paper to write this tribute to a giant—my precious mother, Annie. She had her hardships over the years, as would any parent raising seven children, but she also prayed a lot. That is what made her the giant that she was. A prayer warrior!

I often wondered what made her so strong and courageous. I never understood how she could keep persevering without complaining or shedding a tear. But, if you looked at the life she lived, you would know and understand. Prayer became the conduit to getting her needs met—healing for her family, salvation for her children, provision for the grandchildren, and peace for us all during every storm. She was the thread that held us all together. She taught us to be gracious, loving, kind, hospitable, and considerate of one another and others and how to be respectful.

We were not allowed to wake up without saying good morning. If we ever did, we were made to turn around and go back and do it all over again. She taught us how to cook and clean; boy, did we learn to clean. We would have G.I. parties (I never knew what that meant). These were housecleaning parties, so they were not fun. The first time I heard her say that we were having one, I was excited. I thought we would have cake and ice cream. Wrong! I was handed a mop, a bucket, a sponge, and some Ajax. I was so confused.

We had to clean the crevices of every corner, counter, and cabinet, mop every inch of the floor, wipe every window, and dust every piece of furniture. Whew! I'm exhausted just thinking about it! But, at the end of the day, we all got to see the fruits of our labor. We sat back and enjoyed a sparkling clean abode that anyone would be proud to live in. But still, no cake and ice cream.

Then there's the fact that all seven of us children were druggies. Yep, bona fide druggies. She made us that way. She drugged us to church seven days a week. We were taken to every children's rehearsal, every vacation bible school, every mid-week bible study, every Friday night youth service, and all other goings-on that took place at the church house. We should have all been saints, anointed and dripping in the blood we were at church so much. But that's definitely not our story. That's for an entirely different book. Our lives revolved around long church services and choir rehearsals. Perhaps this is why we didn't get into as much trouble as we could have. I still have mixed feelings about it, though.

Good work ethic was an innate trait of hers. She worked until she retired from Children's Hospital in Los Angeles. So many mornings, she would walk to the bus stop at 5 am to take the long ride across town. She even was held at gunpoint once and robbed. That was scary. From that time, she had one of my brothers walk with her and wait until the bus came. The people at work loved and respected her. She had a great rapport. She made it a point to be on time and work with integrity. During my career, I have tried to emulate her work ethic. It is something that I take great pride in.

I always wanted to give her everything that she would never buy for herself. I wanted her to have the best. She deserved it. I noticed one day that she didn't have a diamond, and I always thought every girl needed diamonds. After all, they are a girl's best friend. The day I gifted her the beautiful cluster diamond cocktail ring, her eyes lit up like the sun. Tears of joy welled up in her eyes that I will never forget. I wanted to capture that look forever. Over the years, I tried to lavish her with good gifts as a way to say thanks for all the sacrifices she had made on my behalf. For all the times I know she went without so that my siblings and I could have. She was the epitome of a good, Godly woman and mother.

I would also notice the look of disappointment when I didn't live up to my potential like she knew I could. Because I wanted to hear her say "I'm so proud of you" and kiss me on my forehead (her kisses were so soft, warm, and endearing), I strove to please her. Yes, I went through my rebellious stage—all teenagers do. But even then, I knew how far to take it if for no other reason than her name being Annie Mae Washington—a woman who didn't play and had eyes in the back of her head. It was the oddest thing. When she called me Kimberly, I knew it was about to go down, most likely me. I was about to go down for something that I had done. There were many of those days, but we don't need to talk about that in this space. Whenever I would call, which was at least once a week, sometimes more, she would answer, "Hello, my Kimberlita!" Never knew why she chose a nickname that made me sound Hispanic. The things that make you go, "hmmm." But no one else had better call me that, or else!

While in her final days, I stayed with her in the hospital. One morning, around 4 am, I awoke to whispers. Initially, I thought it was the nurses coming in, so I sat up quickly so I could hear what they were saying and see what they were doing. To my surprise, there was no one there. Only Mother, lying there speaking to the One. The One who had allowed her to live out her days as a blessed and highly-favored woman. He had brought her, us, a mighty long way—through dangers seen and unseen. I was amazed that even in her dying days, she found the strength to pray. Aah, to have that kind of commitment down to your very last breath.

Though I could go on and on with wonderful accolades about a great woman of God who is so missed, I must say her memory lives on. After a short bout with cancer, the Lord called her home a few years ago. He was merciful and took her rather quickly, so she didn't have to suffer. I am so grateful for that. She is now standing tall with the other great prayer warriors: my grandmother Florence, aunt Gin (Virginia, the preacher teacher), and aunt Fat (Olivia), the great cloud of witnesses cheering me on in the heavens. I am thankful for the legacy of prayer that they have all left. It has truly become my lifeline. No matter where I am or how eloquently someone can exegete a scripture text, I can always hear her saying, in a very matter-of-fact way, "Children, you have to know God for yourself." This is something that she always admonished us to do. So, with this, I dedicate this devotional to you, Mother, my angel, for you are truly the Reasons Why. I wish you were here to read it. I wish I could see the light in your eyes shine once more. Perhaps one day I will. I can't wait. With oceans of love.

Your Kimberlita

When Heaven Speaks
◆◆◆◆◆◆◆◆◆

Introduction

At the age of about nine or ten, I believe I spoke the word of confession, accepting Jesus as my Lord and Savior for the very first time. I was born into the church, meaning my parents were members of that church when my mother gave birth to me. So, I "knew church." But, as a child, I did not fully grasp what it meant to confess all my sins and believe in my heart that Jesus was truly the Son of God and that if I loved my neighbor, no matter what they did or how they treated me, I would be obeying God's commandments; well, at least one of them. All I knew was that God wanted everyone to do it, and if I wanted to live a happy life, then it was not an option not to. Unfortunately, my salvation hung in the balance shortly after that. It may have even vanished completely the day one of my "best friends," Jimmy, flung what felt like a boulder right smack at my right eye. We had been playing at recess, and I stopped, hands on knees, to catch a much-needed breath when suddenly a rock hit me so hard I nearly lost my eye. I remember having to wear this hideous, bulky patch over my eye for what seemed like an eternity. I was angry and hurt, and so were my mother and the principal of South Park Elementary School. Needless to say, my dear friend was suspended even though he didn't intentionally set out to hurt me. I just decided to catch my breath at the wrong time. I can't fully remember, but when my eye got better, or maybe even before that, I think we were friends again. Go figure.

Fast forward to about eighteen or nineteen, I was much more aware of what was at stake for not giving my life wholeheartedly to God. This time when I confessed and rededicated my life, it was going to be for the long haul. Shortly after, God filled me with His Holy Spirit, and life couldn't have been better. I had so much joy—I was excited to be one of His beloved children. I wanted to do all I could for him, including giving. I had zeal!

I am reminded of a particular Sunday a few weeks after my rededication. I was anxious to get to church and give my tithes. I grew up believing in tithing. It seems as if I heard it in my sleep; it was preached so much. I was told tithing was not an option, especially if I wanted God to bless my life. I had been given about twenty dollars; I can't remember from where, but I wanted to be sure God saw me giving and being obedient—that He knew I was a cheerful giver and was serious about my commitment to him. But, when it was time to give it, I couldn't find it! My $2.00 tithes were gone. I recall going into panic mode. God, how could this happen? I was so eager, so on fire for You. I wanted nothing more than to make You happy. Suddenly, I heard a voice say loudly, "Look in the car," it said. I immediately turned around and looked shockingly at the person sitting directly behind me and said, "huh?" How could she know about my tithe, I thought? She looked at me with a puzzled look and replied, "I didn't say anything." It was customary for the musicians to play a song during offering time because we believed that offering was a part of our worship and since we were cheerful givers, the music just kind of solidified the joyous moment. Because of the music, it was sometimes hard to hear if someone were to talk. But, amidst the music, I knew I heard those words, so I resumed my frantic search for my lost treasure. Before long, I heard that same voice again, "It's in the car!" This time, there seemed to be more urgency in the words. This time, I jumped to my feet and looked around again. I was totally confused, but I heeded the voice anyway. I walked outside to the car and looked around inside, and voilà! There were my two dollars—folded in the ash trash where I didn't even remember leaving them.

When I think back on that day, I realize what I heard was heaven speaking, audibly, to a young soul who was bold, confident, eager, and willing to let nothing deter her from pleasing her Daddy-God. Though God often drops things in my spirit, He hasn't spoken audibly to me since that day. I often wonder, was that a one-time deal? Does every new believer get a one-time audible gift from their Heavenly Father? These questions I may never know the answer to. Perhaps I can ask when I meet Him face-to-face. What I do know for sure is that He spoke to me. He spoke to me because that day, in that moment of desperation, my heart was wide open. At that moment, I wanted nothing more than to please him.

While seeking God about this assignment, I was playing a song by Chris McClarney (ft. Hollyn) titled "I'm Listening." It was through those lyrics that I heard God speak the title of this devotional, **When Heaven Speaks**. The words of the song spoke volumes to me and were the very sentiments of my heart. In your quiet time, I encourage you to listen to the words of that song and permit it to minister to you as it did me.

As you journey with me through this 52-week devotional, it is my prayer that you will allow the Word of God to minister to you through the words that He has given me to deliver. Each devotional contains either real-life personal experiences or actual events to help you relate a little better. I encourage you to devote time each day to get into your quiet place and just be still and wait. Wait on the Holy Spirit to instruct you and reveal to you exactly what He intends for you to take away from what you have read. Keep an open mind so you will not miss any truths that He wants to speak to you. And listen for the still, quiet voice within.

That day, as I searched for the tithe I was determined to give, He was the center of my focus. Heaven is eager to speak to us today, but only when He becomes our sole focal point. When heaven has our undivided attention, when all distractions have been put in their proper places, and all other voices have been silenced (with so much going on in our world, that is so much easier said than done), but when we get to the place of total desperation and search for God frantically like the treasure that He is, we will find him. When we surrender to God, then and only then will Heaven speak. And not only will it speak, but it will also open for us, pouring out everything we stand in need of. Allow God to quiet your heart, center your spirit, and align your desires with His will. Shhhh. Pay close attention. Heaven is speaking. Are you listening?

My Inspiration: To speak gratitude is courteous and pleasant, to enact gratitude is generous and noble, but to live gratitude is to touch Heaven.
~ *Johannes A. Gaertner*

Week One

Small Miracle
My testimony Part 1

> *Jesus looked at them and said, "With man this is impossible, but with God all things are possible."*
>
> **Matthew 19:26**

The last week of January 1995 changed my life forever. When the doctors suggested that they induce labor to give my unborn child a better chance at survival, I was afraid, and I just knew, or so I thought I did, that there was no way for him to survive being born so soon. He needed to stay in there! He had more developing and growing to do. If I chose not to, the doctors assured me that the toxins that were building in my body would begin to poison him, and he for sure wouldn't make it. At least this way, he would have a fighting chance. So, there I was, at only 24 weeks gestation, preparing to bring a life into the world.

Is that it? That's all he weighs? Those were the questions I posed to the nurse as she gave the news about the baby boy I had just given birth to—coming in at a whopping 1lb, 5oz! But those weren't the only questions I had. The fear and uncertainty I felt kept me from posing the real question, "Is my baby going to die?" The terror inside wouldn't allow me to formulate the actual words for fear of the possible answer—something no mother wants to ever hear: "Your child didn't make it. We did all we could, but it wasn't enough." The mere thought of it made me utterly sick to my stomach. I couldn't sleep or eat. In all actuality, the desire to do either of those things had left me. All I could think about and wanted was for my baby to be alright.

Coming from a large family, and in my case, the baby of seven, at one point, I kind of expected to get some special privileges because I just figured it came with the title of "being the baby." It's funny, though. Once I became a mother, my focus was no longer on "me." There was an instant shift in my whole thought process once my little one arrived on the scene. All I could think about was him. I thought it was my duty to at least try to do something to ensure he "made it," so I resorted to what I knew best—what had been instilled in me as a child: I prayed and prayed. I even made bargains with God. "God, if you just let him live, you can take me." After all, I did have him out of wedlock. I had sinned, so it was only right that God takes me in exchange for my son. At least, that's what sounded reasonable to me at the time. As I think back on that time, I'm so glad God chose not to listen to my foolish pleas as a remedy to my circumstance. I'm glad that He had a better plan and purpose for both my baby and me. A plan that would not entail me bargaining my life away and making promises that, in retrospect, I have broken so many times. If God had held me to it all, I might not be here to tell this story. Thank God for His mercy!

The ensuing days, weeks, and months brought so much uncertainty. Once Christian, the name God placed in my heart for my little one, was born, they rushed him to Children's Hospital while I stayed at St. Mary's. As if it weren't bad enough that he had to be born so early, now he was being taken away, so I couldn't even see him at all—at least for a while. The truth of the matter is he was never sick or had any issues. However, I was the one with the issues. At the time I gave birth, I had no idea of what had been brewing inside, just how much fluid was building around my lungs. I had pulmonary edema, and it was poisoning my baby! I kept asking myself how this could happen. I thought I took care of us well during the pregnancy, and yet, this. I was puzzled and had convinced myself I was indeed being punished for my sins. I was told by the doctors that if he lived, and it was a big IF, he would have a plethora of issues, including respiratory problems like asthma, a speech impediment, retardation, delayed motor skills, growth, etc. It was all so overwhelming, and I was utterly terrified. All I could do was pray.

(Stay tuned for the conclusion of the story at the beginning of part II)

My Inspiration: Today, look for a small sign, a small miracle, a small thing of beauty that will connect you to the **Source** of all beauty and miracles.

~ Annie Kagan

HEAVEN SPEAKS TO ME: *Name a time in your life when you were in the middle of a difficult circumstance. What was your response? In what ways were you shown support by those around you?*

_____

_____

_____

_____

_____

_____

_____

_____

_____

_____

_____

_____

Scripture Reading: Psalm 146:8; Jeremiah 17:14; 3 John 1:2

PRAYER: Most gracious and kind God, thank you for breathing life into us and our every situation. Thank you for the small life-sustaining miracles that you perform on our behalf every day. Help us not be so busy with living that we miss the blessings of the small miracles, the things that we often take for granted, like waking up with soundness of mind and the good activities of our limbs and the ability to see the miracle of life being lived all around us. Amen!

Week Two

The Calm of My Storm

*Peace I leave with you; my peace I give to you.
Not as the world gives do I give to you. Let not your
Hearts be troubled, neither let them be afraid.*

John 14:27

Growing up in California, my family, friends, and I would often make trips to the bustling shores of the grand Pacific Ocean. The beach became one of my favorite places to go, even to this day. Even though my visits are much less frequent these days, I developed both a fondness and appreciation for its vastness and strength. It somehow seemed to render a sense of calmness for me, no matter how I felt emotionally. I was in total awe at how it all seemed to stay in its rightful place – at least most of the time.

So, I would be at a loss for words when I would hear the news about how hurricanes, typhoons, and storms gone wild would literally obliterate coastal shores and wash away entire cities nearby. It would just stun me. How could something so calming, beautiful, and peaceful be so fierce and angry, causing so much hurt, pain, destruction, and even death?

The storms we sometimes face are very similar. The adversity we experience in life often comes suddenly with fierceness and brutality, as we've never seen before. And, when it catches us off guard, what may have begun as a small thunderstorm has now quickly developed into a hurricane of scheduled events, leaving us scrambling for cover—a place of refuge and safety. Once done, it leaves in its wake a life in pieces. But, no matter how we describe our storm—the trial we encounter in our lives, big or small, rainstorm or typhoon, there is awesome news! Our Heavenly Father makes storm calls, and what's more, He knows exactly where yours is raging. Notice how earlier I mentioned "scheduled events," well, guess what? Though our storm may catch us by surprise, it doesn't catch Him by surprise. He saw your storm brewing from afar. After all, He is the all-knowing, sovereign God, and He is with us even in our lowest moments, our darkest hours, and our deepest despair **(Joshua 1:9)**. He is with us in our every life's storm, waiting to calm, protect, and heal us. His presence gives us hope, reassurance, strength, and peace!

Jesus reassures the disciples that He was leaving His peace with them and that what He was giving them was not as the world would give it—and try to take it back **(verse 27)**. Because of this peace, we do not have to be afraid or let our hearts be troubled. Furthermore, the good news doesn't stop there! Not only is God with us in the storm, but He is also the only one who can calm the rage in our storm. **Mark 14 (verses 35-41)** tells how Jesus rebuked the storm with two powerful words, "Be still," and instantly, the wind ceased and was completely calm. Wow! How awesome is it to get a **Word** from the Lord that has the power to instantaneously change the trajectory of your storm? When things look their bleakest, trusting God wholeheartedly, nothing wavering, will always give us peace in the midst of our every storm.

My Inspiration: I find the great thing in this world is not so much where we stand, as in what direction we are moving: To reach the port of heaven, we must sail sometimes with the wind and sometimes against it – but we must sail, and not drift, nor lie at anchor.
~ Oliver Wendell Holmes, Sr.

HEAVEN SPEAKS TO ME: In what area in your life do you need God to speak a word so you can have the peace He promises?

_____
_____
_____
_____
_____
_____
_____
_____
_____
_____
_____
_____
_____
_____
_____

Scripture Reading: Philippians 4:7, Isaiah 26:3; Psalm 16:8; Proverbs 12:25

PRAYER: Loving and kind God, you are a good, good father! Please grant me peace of mind and calm my troubled heart. My spirit is turbulent like the bustling sea. I can't seem to find balance in any area of my life; therefore, I stumble and worry constantly. Give me the strength and clarity of mind to find my purpose and calling and walk therein the path that you have laid out for my life. Amen!

Week Three

The Blessing in the Press

When she heard about Jesus, she came up behind him In the crowd and touched his cloak, ²⁸ because she thought, "if I just touch his clothes, I will be healed."

Mark 5:27-28

We are moved by many things in life. We feel compelled to act or move a certain way when we consider something worth going after or moving towards. The more value we put on a thing, the harder we tend to work to obtain it. We press our way to what we want. As women, we press our way through college, then we press our way up the rigorous, sometimes dog-eat-dog, and often male-dominated corporate ladders, and then work tirelessly to break through all manner of glass ceilings to try and earn our keep. But how often do we press our way to spiritual fulfillment, to a deeper, more faith-driven understanding of who God is and can be in our lives? How often do we press to wholeness and healing in our broken places? Do we hold back because of pride? Or, because we want to keep up appearances and appear to be on top of our game like we have it going on and all together? That is until our wounds are forcefully exposed by the pressure of our pain, and we have run out of places to hide. It is at this moment that we must press!

In the gospel of **Mark (verses 25-34)**, we read about a woman with a life-altering issue of blood. She bled for 12 long, excruciating years. According to Jewish law, a woman in her condition was considered unclean and was made to be isolated from the rest of the world. I would imagine that, after so many years, she had become anemic and emaciated, which caused her body to be very weak and lifeless. Her limbs had become thin and probably in a skeletal state. She was in a wasted condition and was depicted as a broken outcast! She had nothing more to lose; she had lost it all. After going to so many doctors with no hope of getting better, she had exhausted all other means of being healed. The woman had risked it all with nowhere else to turn but to Jehovah Rapha, the God that heals. Isn't it wonderful to know that even when we come late and make bringing our issues to Jesus the last resort, He is still able and willing to meet us at the point of our needs and turn our issues into triumphs?

The woman, for whatever reason, was not given a name. She was defined by her issue; hence, "the woman with the issue of blood." Perhaps, she was not given a name because Jesus wanted to show us that our names, titles, and statuses mean nothing without our humility and the willingness to allow ourselves to be uncomfortable in the press. Or that her name did not matter as much as the miracle her life and act of faith would represent throughout history. Though her name was never mentioned, her act of faith will forever be etched in the chronicles of biblical history. Furthermore, her desperate press through the crowd was publically recognized just as her public act of faith. Wouldn't you rather be remembered as a woman of faith rather than the household name that quickly climbed the corporate ladder only to find that she is alone and without a savior?! Leviticus 15:25

It was her desperation, not her issue, that made her bold enough to press her way through the crowd to her blessing of healing. Had she continued to allow herself to be a prisoner to her issue, she would have remained too weak to press past her pain and inability. Because God is sensitive to His children's needs, when He sees us operating in our faith, it touches Him in a special way, and He becomes eager to respond. So, as she leaned in and touched Jesus' hem, a virtue of healing left His body. When He asked, "who touched me?" (I can hear her saying in her weakened state, "It's me, it's me, it's me, oh Lord standing in need...") she, trembling in her voice, fessed up to touching His hem. As quickly as the virtue of healing left Him, so quickly did her countenance change from distraught to unexplainable joy and eternal gratitude. What a testimony! A woman, once unnamed and emaciating for 12 years, was now made completely whole, strengthened, and restored in an instant. Though the law of that day clearly stated that if an unclean woman even touched someone else while flowing, that person would also become unclean **(Leviticus 15:25)**. But through the sacrifice of Jesus, the penalties for violating the law were eradicated and what was once contaminated to the world had no effect on Jesus the Christ. So, instead of the woman making those around her unclean in the crowd with her issue, He made her clean despite her issue! It no longer had her trapped and bound to a near-lifeless existence.

    Her healing was not, as the story suggests, due to her touching the hem of Jesus's garment. It was her enormous faith that touched Him. Her faith captured the Healer's attention, and He was moved to action. It was her faith that made her whole!

My Inspiration: When I look back on my life, I see pain, mistakes, and heartache. When I look in the mirror, I see strength, learned lessons, and pride in myself.
~ **Author Unknown**

When Heaven Speaks

HEAVEN SPEAKS TO ME: What things have you been desperate to obtain in your life that has taken the place of your fervency for obtaining more of God? In what ways are you willing to press to obtain the wholeness your life's issues need? How will you press to obtain more of God?

_____
_____
_____
_____
_____
_____
_____
_____
_____
_____
_____

Scripture Reading: Zechariah 8:23, Philippians 3:14; 1 Corinthians 9:25, 1 Timothy 6:12

PRAYER: Dear Lord, I thank you for being an ever-present help in time of need. I am crying out to you today, Heavenly Father, as I have exhausted all other means. Forgive me for seeking help in other places first and making you the last resort. I ask that you would renew my spirit and make me whole in every area of my life. My heart yearns to find your comforting presence amid my issue(s). I am broken, shattered, and dismayed. Pick me up and plant my feet on solid ground and grant me your tender mercies. Amen!

Week Four

The Great Exchange

For he hath made him to be sin for us, who knew no sin; That we might be made the righteousness of God in him.

2 Corinthians 5:21

To say, I am a movie watcher would be an understatement. I am an *avid* movie watcher, to say the least, and I enjoy action and suspense thrillers. Often I have watched movies where the government or the good guys (not that they are synonymous) would be put in a position where they would have to make a deal with the bad guys to get one of their good guys to safety. The majority of the time, something would go awry, and the deal would be a bust. Some tough guy cop, FBI, or CIA agent would swing through saving the day so that the bad guys get to go to jail and the good guys get to go home to their anxiously waiting families, having never been the wiser of what their loved one just experienced to be able to see their smiling faces once more.

When Jesus chose to die on Calvary, he exchanged his holy being for our sinful life. Can you imagine being loved so much that someone would be willing to die for you? I have heard so many people say that "it seems that the good always dies young" or that "it's always the good people that bad things happen to." Well, this is certainly true with Jesus Christ. Though he was fully human, He was also sinless, unlike his fellow humankind. We were flawed in every sense of the word. We had fallen from grace in the garden and were forever separated from the Father until

He sent His only begotten Son to die for our many transgressions so that we could someday be reconciled with Him.

From the beginning, Jesus always knew what his purpose for being made flesh was. He came to live as the perfect example and die as the ultimate sacrifice. When he was betrayed and sent to die on an old rugged cross, he could have easily sent for his angels to come and save the day. But, he knew that in doing so, he would not fulfill the promise of the Father. He knew that if the angels rescued him, humanity as we know, it would be forever lost and without hope. We would forever be separated from our Heavenly Father—we would be at a point of no return. If you were put in a similar situation, would you exchange your life for a bunch of folks you didn't even know? Could you even do it for those you do know? Well, He does know us —every one of us. In fact, He knows each strand of hair on our heads **(Luke 12:7)** and has deemed us as valuable and worth dying for! God knew we needed a redeemer, so He exchanged His only son for a dying world. His son Jesus exchanged his life to be the propitiation for our sins. He became wrath so that we would not have to experience the Father's judgment for our iniquities. Thank God for Jesus!

Even today, in our everyday life, Jesus is still making exchanges. Whatever situation you may find yourself in at this very moment, allow him to make the exchange without resistance. He can trade your pills for his peace, your hopelessness for hope in Him, your fears for his courage, and all your weaknesses for His strength.

My Inspiration: The price of anything is the amount of life you exchange for it
~ **Henry David Thoreau**

HEAVEN SPEAKS TO ME: In what ways can we, as Christians, remain cognizant of the great sacrifice Jesus made on our behalf? Can you think of some of the ways that we often crucify him all over again because of our disobedience?

_____

_____

_____

_____

_____

_____

_____

_____

_____

_____

_____

_____

Scripture Reading: Romans 8:3-4, John 3:16-17; Hebrews 9:12; 1 Timothy 2:5; Isaiah 53:1-12

PRAYER: Great redeemer, I thank you for the undeserving sacrifice made on that old rugged cross on my behalf. Help me to present my body as a living sacrifice that is acceptable to you as a reminder of the great love you have for me and the price you paid so I could have eternal life through your son Jesus. Amen!

Week Five

My Giants, God's Armor

◆◆◆◆◆◆◆◆◆◆

David said to the Philistine, "You come against me with a sword and spear and javelin, but I come against you in the name of the Lord Almighty, the God of the armies of Israel, whom you have defied. [46] This day the LORD will deliver you into my hands....

1 Samuel 17:45-46

Have you ever heard it said that someone brought a knife to a gunfight? That is usually said when someone is out-matched, whether due to size, numbers, resources, or ability. Naturally, you would say that with a gunfight simply because of the power, speed, and overall magnitude of impact a gun's bullet would impose upon its target as opposed to a knife. Though sharp and capable of inflicting much pain with deep cuts, a knife is just simply no match. Though both can be deadly, somehow, the whole thought of being hit by a speeding bullet is frightening in and of itself, let alone feeling the impact of one.

If you have ever attended a Sunday school class as a child, you have undoubtedly heard the story of David and Goliath. For a brief second, let's use our vivid imaginations to compare the two. Like a mouse is to an elephant, that's how small David was to Goliath! Well, maybe that's a bit too vivid, but you get the gist, though, right? Talk about an unfair advantage!

In man's eyes, David was, in no way, shape, form, or fashion, a match for an angry giant with an ax to grind, or any giant for that matter. All odds were against him, yet he trusted the (his) Almighty God to deliver him by declaring, "I come against you in the name of the Lord Almighty; this day, the LORD will deliver you (Big Giant) into my hands."

When was the last time you spoke with authority to the Giants in your life? What would happen if you demanded that the mountains that seem unmovable be moved in the name of your God Almighty? Whether now or in the recent past, we have all had giants try and invade our lives with hostile takeovers. What's your giant's name? Is it fear, anxiety, or low self-image? Are you plagued by the ego monster, pride, and self-centeredness? Or are you dealing with a health giant that has left your future looking bleak? Perhaps yours has you drowning in debt? The list could go on and on, but no matter what your giants are, God has and is the answer! Isaiah tells us, "No weapon formed against us shall prosper" (54:17). And then, in chapter 59, he gives us another assurance when he says, "When the enemy comes against us like a flood, the Spirit of the Lord shall lift up a standard against him" (vs. 19 KJV).

There is a myriad of scriptures with promises and reassurances that God will indeed come to our aid in the time of need. But, there are times when we must go into our spiritual survival mode and reach for the *dunamis* power that lies within us. The meaning of *dunamis* in Greek is the "Explosive power of God or the dynamic ability of God." The great thing about *dunamis* power is that it never has anything at all to do with our personal strength or ability. But rather, it refers to God Almighty's power working through us. And it is this power alone that keeps us while developing our character as we glorify Him in faith and activate the authority to not only slay but enslave the giants in our lives.

Those enslaved giants are now at our command and must yield to the Power and Authority that is now working through us! So, with *dunamis* power, I can speak to the mountains and giants in my life, no matter what they are or how big they appear, and with authority, tell them to move and be gone from me! It was that power working in David that enabled him to slay Goliath, and it's that same power working in us today that allows us to put the giants in our lives under our feet where they belong, for good!

My Inspiration: The giant in front of you is never bigger than the GOD who is in you
~ **MMA Armored**

HEAVEN SPEAKS TO ME: What do the giants in your life look like? In what ways have you learned to allow God to fight those giants? We know that having the right armor when in war is vital to obtaining victory. What kind of armor do you put on when you are in spiritual warfare?

_____
_____
_____
_____
_____
_____
_____
_____
_____
_____
_____
_____
_____

Scripture Reading: Ephesians 6:11; 2 Corinthians 6:7; 1 Thessalonians 5:8; Isaiah 59:17

PRAYER: My God, the mighty warrior! I thank you for all the battles you have won on my behalf. In those times when my natural strength weans and I feel like I can't win, you always step in and fight for me. Father, You are my strong tower in whom I can run and find refuge. Amen!

<u>Week Six</u>

Blinded to See

He answered, "Whether he is a sinner I do not know. One thing I do know, that though I was blind, now I see."

John 9:25

Hymnals could be found behind every pew in both my aunt's and uncle's churches. They were both pastors of African Methodist Episcopal churches. At each service, especially on Sundays, the glorious sounds of the hymns of old would ring out from parishioners singing in all manner of notes, ranges, and tones. But, it always seemed that they would sing certain songs, the more popular ones, louder than others.

Whenever John Newton's "Amazing Grace" was in the song line-up, I knew it was going to be a hallelujah time! The line, "I once was lost, but now am found, I was blind, but now I see," was probably the most well-known line of the whole hymn. Even as a young woman, I could tell it was sung with such conviction, like the one singing it had experienced it for themselves. Though I can't be for certain, perhaps they had experienced something that I hadn't quite been privy to yet. What I do know for sure is that when they sang that particular hymn, the atmosphere changed, and there was rarely a dry eye in the building. Given the ages of most, I am sure their life experiences have taught them many a lesson. Some, I would imagine, were life-altering.

Paul (who at this time was still Saul), on the road to Damascus, was on his way to persecute the Christians when suddenly he was approached by God, a bright light from heaven, who confronted him about his motives by asking him "Why do you persecute me?" Paul then acknowledged Him as Lord and asked who He was. The reply was, "I am Jesus whom thou persecutest" (Acts 1:5). Scripture informs us that this was solely a personal experience because those traveling on the road with him neither saw nor heard anything (v. 7). It was at this point that Paul was without sight.

Most people believe that Paul's conversion to Christianity and his name change all took place on the road to Damascus. However, in scripture, we are told a much different story. Upon arriving in Damascus, he was given further instruction and would soon receive a message from Ananias, a messenger from God who not only restored his sight but also instructed him to "Arise, and be baptized, and wash away thy sins, calling on the name of the Lord" (Acts 22:16). So, the truth of the matter is that Paul was not saved until his sight was restored and he was baptized in the city of Damascus, not on the road to Damascus.

So, what does this tell us? Oftentimes God may have to allow something drastic to take place in our lives to get our attention and bring us to our senses so we can experience a real turning point. Then and only then can He perform the miracle of conversion and make us true disciples, turning us from an enemy of God to an advocate for Him!

Each person's "coming to Jesus" experience is different, dependent on how stubborn we are and just how willing we are to surrender our carnal will to His divine will for our lives. Unless God intervenes by His grace, we will go through our lives blinded by our sins, condemnation, and shame. But, God, whose magnitude of love for us is so great that He will deliver us right when we are about to self-destruct.

His love is too great to leave us in the sinful and hopeless state that we so often find ourselves in. So, if you are in a dark period in your life and can't seem to see your way, let the bright light of the Holy Spirit shine in your life and let it change you from the inside out. Allow the Light to restore your sight so that you can see the beauty that awaits a life well lived in Christ Jesus. When the Light of Jesus shines, you will be amazed at the great works you can do, just like Paul.

My Inspiration: The eyes are useless when the mind is blind
~ *Unknown*

HEAVEN SPEAKS TO ME: Recall your "coming to Jesus" moment; in what drastic way(s) did God have to get your attention? How has that experience changed your life for the better? How can you use that experience to impact others?

_____

_____

_____

_____

_____

_____

_____

_____

_____

_____

_____

_____

_____

_____

_____

_____

Scripture Reading: Acts 2:38; Mark 16:16: Galatians 3:26-28; 1 Corinthian 2:10-15; John 6:29

PRAYER: Sovereign God, thank you for being in my blind spot and for guiding me when I couldn't see you because of the sin I allowed to enter my life. Shine your bright light of salvation amid my sin so that my path is illuminated by your great grace and your tender mercies. Amen!

Week Seven

Well-Watered

*....If thou knewest the gift of God, and who it is that saith to thee,
Give me to drink; thou wouldest have asked of Him, and he would
have given thee living water.*

John 4:10

I am no one's gardener by any means. My thumbs are not green in the least bit. They are probably more like blue-black when it comes to making things grow. However, knowing that fact did not keep me from several failed attempts at maintaining a few well-cared-for houseplants. I had peace lilies whose thirst was revealed when their leaves began to droop, and that was my cue that a drink of water was needed.

But somehow, I would either water them too much or too little or I would give them too much sun or perhaps not enough of it. I just couldn't seem to get it right, that is, until one day, I was suddenly struck with a lightning bolt of common sense – ask the Googler! When I began to read up on how to take care of houseplants, one of the things I learned was that not all water is created equal.

It is recommended that you not use distilled or tap water to water your houseplants. Tap water sometimes has too many harmful chemicals and can cause fluoride build-up in the soil, which will stress the plant. Though distilled water can be used, it's simply not effective; it's just dead water. Everything has been removed through the boiling and evaporation process, which means all the good minerals have been boiled away. To my surprise, though, the best water for houseplants is spring water and good old rainwater! Rainwater is said to be tops in purity for plant watering, and it helps the plants to grow tall, healthy, and proud!

As I came to this realization, I was reminded of just how refreshing rainwater could be. It made me think back as a child and how refreshing it was to play in the rain. It didn't matter how drenched we were — those were fun times. How refreshing it was, especially on a hot summer day, to feel the rejuvenating pellets of heavenly rainfall on my sun-scorched face. When we feel drained from all the hustling and bustling of our busy lives and our proverbial well has run dry, we must allow ourselves to be reminded of our need for the restoring power of God's heavenly rain. In the story of the woman at the well, Jesus offered the thirsty woman a drink from a well that never runs dry and assured her that if she drank from His well, she would never thirst again!

Life has a rotten way of depleting us of our hope, strength, courage, and at times our faith. However, God has given us promises that we can stand and rely on when our circumstances become overwhelming. It was never our creator's intention for us to be dried up with an "I'm just gonna keep trying but never really getting there" kind of existence. He created us to be well-watered Christians who regularly draw from the strength of his son's well of living water and who find our wholeness and joy solely in Him alone.

We do not need to look to the world and all its alluring possessions to give us the feeling of fulfillment. That feeling is only temporal (2 Cor. 4:18). Our fulfillment is in God, for his way is perfect (2 Sam. 22:31). He is the only one who can quench our thirst and satisfy our every need. Instead of thirsting for worldly things, we should ask God to give us an insatiable desire for more of him. He does not want to just pacify our thirst as the distilled water did for my houseplants, but He wants to truly satisfy our thirsty souls with a drenching of his Holy Spirit that strengthens our inner person, gives us confidence in his Holy Being, and increases our faith in his sovereignty.

My Inspiration: And one day she discovered that she was fierce. And strong. And full of fire. And that not even she could hold herself back because her passion burned brighter than her fears
~ **Mark Anthony**

HEAVEN SPEAKS TO ME: What temporal things have you thirsted for? How can we, as Christians, turn our worldly thirst into an insatiable thirst for more of the things of God?

_____

_____

_____

_____

_____

_____

_____

_____

_____

_____

_____

_____

_____

_____

_____

Scripture Reading: 2 Corinthians 4:18, 2 Samuel 22:31; Isaiah 44:3; 1 Corinthians 12:13

PRAYER: Lord, this world can be so tempting with all the things that appeal to our flesh, and if we are not careful, we will fall prey to its allure. Help me instead to develop an insatiable hunger and thirst for You, and let my appetite be for more of the living water that flows from your Holy word. Amen!

Week Eight

No Parking Zone

◆◆◆◆◆◆◆◆◆

I know that I still have a long way to go. But there is one thing I do: I forget what is in the past and try as hard as I can to reach the goal before me. I keep running hard toward the finish line to get the prize that is mine....

Philippians 3:13-14, ERV

Life can be funny sometimes, whether you have a sense of humor or not. No matter how hard we try, our past has a way of catching up to us and reminding us of every hurt, disappointment, and mistake that we ever encountered. But, in living this maze called life, I've learned that despite our most desperate attempts, we can't erase, deny, outrun, or escape our past. It has the propensity to show up at the most inopportune times, mostly at times when we have convinced ourselves that we have somehow buried it all under about a thousand miles beneath the surface of our "calm" lives. However, with God as our compass, He can help us navigate our lives so that our past does not imprison us and keep us from reaching the promises that await us in our tomorrow.

I like what Paul had to say about forgetting the things that are behind us and pressing as hard as we possibly can to reach the goal of our tomorrow (vs. 13). In other words, though our yesterday is not as important as our tomorrow, it is certainly the conduit that gets us there.

The pain we endured along our journey is the catalyst that will catapult us to our destiny, so we can't afford to park anywhere, much less at the points where we experienced pain. If you allow yourself to park at the point of your pain, you will deny the world the opportunity to see the wonderful works God wants to do through you. The only place you should be parking is at your final destination, which is with your Heavenly Father, who has already prepared a place for you. (John 14:3). In the place He has prepared, you can rest assured that you won't need to worry about the hurt, sadness, sorrow, sickness, or disease of your yesterday. We can worship and praise our Father for giving us the strength to endure the heartache regardless of our past and filling our hearts with the joy and peace that only He can give.

Being able to move forward isn't always an easy undertaking, but God certainly wants to take you there. He wants to heal you from the inside so the world outside can see what He has done through you and will do through them also. When tragedy hits you like a big Mack truck, and it feels like all the wind has been knocked right out of you and you suffer loss—whether a job, child, divorce, or death of a close friend as a result of sickness, the confusion, and distraction of it all—it can stop you dead in your tracks.

It's at times like these when moving forward almost seems virtually impossible, but do not allow yourself to be trapped in a moment in time. The many scars and bruises of your past do not change who you are in Christ! There is ministry inside of you that needs to be cultivated and spread throughout the world. So, just know that every forward step of faith that you take gets you that much closer to your place of wholeness and healing.

Forget the former things and don't look back (Isa. 43:18-19). Don't let yourself die at the place where you chose to park because you refused to trust God with your past. Know that God is not punishing you. He is preparing you. Trust His plan and not your pain. Permit God to rescue and restore you for the wonderful journey ahead, so you don't miss out on the best life He has to offer you through his son Jesus Christ!

My Inspiration: *I never knew how strong I was until I had to forgive someone who wasn't sorry, and accept an apology I never received.*
~ Author Unknown

HEAVEN SPEAKS TO ME: Take a moment and think back over your life. What things in your past can you think of that might be holding you hostage? What are some actions you can take to help you move forward?

_____
_____
_____
_____
_____
_____
_____
_____
_____
_____
_____
_____
_____
_____
_____

Scripture Reading: Zephaniah 1:12; Proverbs 23:17-18; Jeremiah 29:11; Daniel 9:13

PRAYER: Kind God, forgive me for allowing myself to be a victim of my past. Help me to confront my past with courage and embrace the future you have for me with strong faith. Don't allow me to take up residence at the points of the pain in my past. Thank you for giving me hope and a future in You. Amen!

<u>Week Nine</u>

From Pieces to Peace

The steadfast of mind You will keep in perfect peace, Because he trusts in You

Isaiah 26:3

I can recall a point and time in my life when I felt as if I had been robbed of my peace. I was tormented to the point that I could not sleep. My heart constantly palpitated as if it were going to jump out of my chest at any moment. I lived in fear and anxiety. Life was miserable. Although I must admit, my lack of peace had everything to do with me being out of the will of God, wanting to do things my way and in my timing. I had been disobedient in an area that I knew I had been given explicit instructions on, and yet, there I was being harassed by the one who also knew my instructions-the enemy!

During that period, if someone had told me that the results of my decisions would have cost me my peace of mind, I would not have believed them. I was convinced that I knew what was best and that the decision(s) I made would have a high yield of everything I wanted. Wrong. I remember crying and spending a lot of time thinking about what could have possibly gone wrong in the planning process. It was always instilled in me to pray about everything. Prayer was the conduit to getting things done in the spirit realm and the natural also. However, when I "prayed," I was only focused on the natural and what my fleshly desires were. I was carnal in my thinking, and my prayers were also carnal. Because I chose to disregard what I knew about God and his word, every decision I made seemed to strip me of my peace little by little. My life started to feel like it had a python hold on me. Like I was wrapped in the coils of its strength in an attempt to squeeze the life right out of me. I was losing air. I couldn't breathe. Once it started to loosen its grip, what was left was a bag of broken pieces - fragments of who I was created to be.

I know I am not alone when I say life can be unrelenting. At times, it simply doesn't play fair. It takes courage to be intentional and live our life the way God intends. And so it is when it comes to the things of God and being obedient to his specific instructions. Not obeying is not an option. When God gives us purpose and mandates us to walk out that calling, it's not always easy. But, what I found out the hard way is that though we may want what God calls us to do to be easy, He doesn't call us to ease: he calls us to destiny. Until we learn to operate in sync with Him and what He is trying to do in and through our lives, we will never obtain the peace He promised us.

There is a song whose lyrics say, "The safest place in the whole wide world is in the will of God." Those words could not be truer. The feeling you get when you know that you have obeyed God renders peace like none other. I love what Psalm 91 (NIV) has to say, *"He who dwells in the shelter of the Most High will rest in the shadow of the Almighty. I will say of the LORD, He is my refuge and my fortress, my God, in whom I trust. Surely he will save you from the fowler's snare and from the deadly pestilence."* What this tells us is that as long as we are in His will, not our own, we are sheltered by heaven's covering. Furthermore, we have heaven's rest and its protection from sickness and disease and salvation from the enemy's clutches. I don't know about you, but if I have all that, I know I have Peace in Jesus.

The next time we decide to go off on our tangents and do things our way without seeking God's will or blatantly ignoring God's specific instructions, be reminded that when we don't heed God's call, we inadvertently leave the door wide open for the thief to come in and steal our peace, kill our joy and try to destroy our destiny. Remind Satan of who you are in Christ. Be courageous and take heart, knowing that to be in the will of God is truly the safest and most peaceful place in the whole wide world to be.

My Inspiration: Ego says: "Once everything falls into place, I will find peace." Spirit says: "Find peace and everything will fall into place."
~ **Author Unknown**

HEAVEN SPEAKS TO ME: Have you ever been without peace? What effect did it have on you? Can you identify the cause? What did you do to regain your peace? What will you do going forward?

_____
_____
_____
_____
_____
_____
_____
_____
_____
_____
_____
_____

Scripture Reading: Revelation 21:4, Psalm 34:18, John 16:33, Ephesians 2:14, Psalm 147:3

PRAYER: Merciful Lord. You are the mender of broken hearts and lives. Thank you for putting my life back together again. I am so grateful that you helped me to pick up all those broken pieces that had been scattered and helped me to make sense of them all in light of Your truth. May I forever embrace and walk in wholeness and holiness. Amen!

Week Ten

Sheltering in Place

Be still, and know that I am God: I will be exalted Among the heathen, I will be exalted in the earth." The Lord of hosts is with us; the God of Jacob is our refuge.

Psalm 46:10-11

By nature, I am what is called a worrywart. It's not something I'm proud of, and I must say that God has blessed me to grow in that area over the years. However, sometimes I still get a little anxious about things that are not moving forward fast enough for me. I can recall many times in my life when I moved too quickly or in haste, only to find that I screwed up badly because of my impatience.

If only I had waited a little longer; or if only I had thought this through a little more; or if I should have sought wise counsel before making that move. If you're honest, we have all made similar haphazard decisions that we ended up regretting, only to find that God has ways and means of getting our attention, slowing us down, and making us "see the light" or at least see things more clearly.

For most of us, being still because we just want to is a lot different than being made to do so. Because of our rebellious nature, we tend to resent being told what to do and when. Sit still, be quiet, stay home, or keep your distance are all commands that we, in America, simply can't seem to get used to. However, such mandates force us to look at our lives in new ways.

It gives us glimpses of the hurriedness of our lives from new vantage points. All the things we overlooked. The times we said we didn't have time to spend with a friend in need. The games we told our kids we couldn't make. Quality time with our spouses we didn't fulfill. All the broken promises. The list could go on and on. We have been MIA, missing in action, for years all because we have been too busy to notice the important things – the things that have been right in front of us all along.

Now that circumstances have been changed, the tables have been turned, and the things we were once so sure of, we are now in a state of panic in the middle of a pandemic. The level of trust we had in our cushy jobs and the luxurious homes we barely lived in are now something we fear losing – in addition to our lives. But, for those of us who are in a covenant relationship with our Heavenly Father, we are reassured in knowing that if we trust God in the NOW, He will most certainly take care of us in our LATER!

We can trust him with the things we cannot control. The things we can't always identify but fear nonetheless. The uncertainty of the loss of income and material possessions keeps us restless, and the loss of a loved one sends our world into a tailspin. God desires intimacy with his children. He is never too busy to hear us and answer us. He never has a meeting that takes the place of time spent with his most prized possession, nor does he have a business luncheon that lures him away from the parent-teacher conference at his child's school.

He readily avails himself at all times to meet our needs. He is a jealous God (*Exodus 20:5*), and when we put other things in his place and we don't value what he values, then He must respond and remind us of who He is. He is God almighty! The sovereign King! The creator of every being! He is the Great I Am! Our provider, healer, and protector! Take the time to be still and reflect on who God STILL is in your life. Be intentional about reminding your family and friends of who God is - the one who is NEVER too busy for his beloved children. Shelter in the place wherever God is and permit the healing powers of his divine presence to touch the places in your life that nothing else can.

My Inspiration: Don't let people pull you into their STORM. Pull them into your PEACE
~ *Unknown*

HEAVEN SPEAKS TO ME: Have you ever made a decision without consulting God or wise counsel? How did it make you feel? How did the decision affect you? Your family? In what ways does God's word assure us that His peace will be with us?

_____
_____
_____
_____
_____
_____
_____
_____
_____
_____
_____
_____
_____

Scripture Reading: Psalm 91:1; Proverbs 16:7; John 16:33; Isaiah 55:12

PRAYER: Almighty God of peace, thank you for your promise of peace if I keep my mind stayed on you. Give me wisdom in all of my decision-making and help me to seek wise counsel before making a move instead of acting haphazardly. Let me always acknowledge you in all of my ways so that you will be the only one directing my path. Amen!

Week Eleven

A Sun-Scorched Land

The Lord will guide you always; he will satisfy your needs in a sun-scorched land and will strengthen your frame. You will be like a well-watered garden, like a spring whose waters never fail.

Isaiah 58:11, NIV

I watched a movie once that was filmed somewhere in an Indian desert. The scene that most stood out was when a man who had been held captive was thrown out of a moving car and left in the scorching hot desert. Amid his pleas for them not to leave him, he was seen kicking the sand and turning franticly from east to west, trying to decide which way to go. He began walking and walking until his pace began to slow, and his strides shortened as he began to stagger as if he were intoxicated.

Suddenly, in the far distance, he saw what appeared to be water, so he ran as fast as he could, only to find it to be a mirage. By now, he had started to succumb to the heat, and his face and lips started to peel; he was extremely dehydrated, and the heat from the scorching sun was killing him. Finally, he saw what appeared to be an even larger mirage, much bigger than the previous one, but he was determined not to be fooled again. In total despair, he fell to the ground with hopelessness and then breathed his last breath. The sad part about this story is that if only he had taken five more steps, he would have found a pond with cool, refreshing water, and just down the hill, a few more steps was an entire city! He had come so far only to miss his second chance by mere inches.

How often have we traveled through the arid seasons of our lives frantically looking for anything to quench our thirst and ease the pain of being in the "nothing zone" of life, not knowing which way to go? When we go through the dry seasons of our lives and are hit with one devastating thing after another, these valley experiences can seem to last an eternity. We run through life looking for any kind of relief, something that will ease the pain and sometimes numbness of our current circumstances.

We find ourselves indulging in activities that are far removed from the values that we know to be true. We embrace beliefs that only appease our dry places instead of giving life to them. Why do we find it easier to entertain the "status quo" rather than break free of the barriers and strongholds that keep us bound? The enemy of our souls knows and understands that nothing grows in dry, arid places. His goal is to keep us stuck as if in quicksand and make us feel like our only option is to succumb to the thing that is so forcefully dragging us downward. But thanks be to God, our high priest, that He is not a God that can't feel (or be touched with) the infirmities of his people! (Hebrews 4:15).

God knows where we are because, in the person of Christ, He, too, was faced with all kinds of adversity and was tempted, just like us. He understands our struggles, and if we allow Him, He will be in our struggle with us. The phrase "be touched with" comes from the Greek word *sumpatheo*, which is to share an experience with someone or to sympathize with and have compassion for someone. How comforting and reassuring is that thought? To have the almighty God step into our situation and share and identify with our every experience in life is such an awesome thing.

He has compassion for you even in your dry, sun-scorched places because He has been where you are and has felt what you may be feeling at this very moment —

every emotion, disappointment, frustration, and temptation. And since He overcame, so can we because he will never leave nor forsake us. Therefore, we can remain fertile even during a famine! In that, we can put all of our trust.

My Inspiration: God's work done in God's way will never lack God's provision
~ **Hudson Taylor**

HEAVEN SPEAKS TO ME: How does it make you feel knowing that Jesus endured the same trials and temptations that we face today? How does it change the way you respond when going through the dry places in your life? In what ways can you encourage others in their arid seasons of life?

_____

_____

_____

_____

_____

_____

_____

_____

_____

_____

_____

Scripture Reading: Hebrews 4:15, Deuteronomy 31:8, 1 Peter 5:7; Job 38:41; Luke 12:24

PRAYER: God, thank you for being my high priest. Thank you for showing up in my circumstances. Help me to constantly remind myself that you are walking with me in the dry, sun-scorched seasons of my life. Father, thank you for understanding the things I am faced with and that I can bring all my concerns to you boldly and confidently to obtain mercy and find grace in times of need, knowing that I am never alone in the struggle. Amen!

Week Twelve

Good Trouble

*It is the Lord who goes before you.
He will be with you; he will not leave you or forsake you.
Do not fear or be dismayed.*

Deuteronomy 31:8

As a very captivating civil rights legend, friend, and co-laborer of the late great Dr. Martin Luther King Jr., state representative John R. Lewis has left quite an astounding legacy for those left behind to build upon. He was a towering figure who marched with Dr. King in Selma during the civil rights era. When his celebration of life service was being televised, images of him being beaten by police during that march were difficult to watch — for anyone who had any semblance of humanity, that is. Those clips reminded us of the sacrifices he made and was still willing to make up until his very death.

As anyone who has ever heard that name knows, he coined the term "Good Trouble." During his home- going service, there was nothing but wonderful accolades spoken by dignitaries from around the country as well as by three former Presidents of the United States, family, and friends. What a way to be honored! Included with the praises for all his accomplishments were the resounding words, Good Trouble, and how he loved getting into it. Though the phrase may sound like an oxymoron to most, the meaning it carried was everything but contradictory. What he was encouraging people to do was to fight for their human and civil rights no matter the cost. Every speech he gave, like Dr. King, was a call to action because, after all, you just can't leave it up to someone else to fight for what is rightfully yours.

If the truth is told, I've never personally fought for civil rights by protesting and marching, but those who have gone before me and trail-blazed have, and I am forever indebted to them for their courage and commitment. Like today, those who lived in the bible days were all too familiar with the atrocities of the day. We know that there is so much going on in our world, and, unfortunately, not everyone is fighting for peace and the good trouble of insisting on change and equality for all of God's children. For those individuals, we who are in Christ will pray that they will come to know the amazing love of Christ Jesus, who equally loves us all and offers the same great gift of salvation. But, even though there are a plethora of distressing things occupying the headlines and our minds, we can refocus from the trouble brought on by disobedience and blatant disrespect for God's word to the good trouble that He leads us to – the trouble that will ultimately lead to salvation and liberty in Christ Jesus.

In today's society, people seem to be more prone to following people rather than Jesus Christ. They long for the trouble that leads to shame and anguish for those that may be different from them, which ultimately leads to more trouble. They are not willing to put their reputations, careers, and social statuses on the line in the name of sharing the love of Christ. But, scripture tells us that *"He that wins a soul to Christ is wise "(Proverbs 11:30)*. When we long for the trouble that will lead to winning more souls to the Kingdom, we will gain wisdom from God, and our lives will be fulfilled.

My Inspiration: Ah, but a man's reach should exceed his grasp, or what's a heaven for?
~ Robert Browning

HEAVEN SPEAKS TO ME: Name a time when you have fought for something to help others? What was your motivation? Do you feel that God was pleased with the outcome?

_____

_____

_____

_____

_____

_____

_____

_____

_____

_____

_____

_____

Scripture Reading: Proverbs 18:10, Psalm 27:1, John 16:33; Proverbs 28:1; Acts 28:31; 1 John 5:14

PRAYER: Strong and mighty God, thank you for empowering me to be the change that I want to see on the earth. Allow me to work each day in the power and authority you have given me. Help me to invoke change and do it with love and humility. Amen!

Week Thirteen

For My Good and God's Glory

And we know that all things work together for good to them that love God, to them who are the called according to his purpose.

Romans 8:28

I can't begin to count the times that I have sat and allowed my mind to think in retrospect over my life and reminded myself why it was so necessary for me to go through all that I've been through. I know you will agree with me when I say no one wants to experience hurt and disappointment. However, it is those very experiences that have made us into the strong, fearless women that we are today. Whether it was from a failed relationship, the loss of a loved one, job, or friend, or maybe even a life-altering diagnosis, these life events had a purpose whether we saw them as such or not; they were for our good and our making.

But what happens when a business deal goes awry or when you are passed over, repeatedly, for the promotion that you knew without a doubt you are more than qualified for? After all, you pay your tithes and give offerings; you even donate to charity from time to time – doesn't that count for something? How does not getting the job equate to God pouring you out blessings you won't have room to receive (Malachi 3:10)? You may think it doesn't, but it does. You just have to allow yourself to see your circumstances through the lenses of a sovereign God.

We read in Romans that God can work all things together for our good, but for those who love Him and are called according to His purpose. Did you catch that? He takes bad outcomes and turns them into good works for those who both love him and are called, not just went, according to his purpose. In other words, He is sovereignly orchestrating good things concerning you during your painful circumstances in the heavenly realm and turning completely around what was meant for evil and making it all good for His people and His glory (Genesis 50:20). He works out every one of our life's events according to the divine counsel of His sovereign will. That is such great news!

As the finite creatures that we are, there is no way possible for us to know all the hidden things in the mind of an infinite, sovereign God. We can seek Him for His plans for our own lives, and there may even be times when He may reveal things concerning others. However, when we are in our painful realities, it's sometimes difficult to understand what's going on in our world, let alone someone else's world. We can only search the scriptures and stay before God in prayer for his perfect and revealed will for our lives.

James tells us that every good and perfect gift comes from above, coming down from the Father of lights, with whom is no shadow of turning (1:17). Every good thing God gives us he gives not just out of his goodness, but he gives it for our good. Everything God gives or allows us to have and experience in our lives is strategically designed for our good and His glory, even when it doesn't seem like it. The gifts he gives are always perfect. They are exactly what we need, and at the exact moment, we need them. Like his good, and perfect gifts, his timing is also perfect- not a minute too soon or a moment too late.

God is only glorified when we have obediently surrendered to his perfect will for our lives – no grumbling or complaining, just total surrender. We must adhere to the commandments of God through the grace his son Jesus provides, honor, praise, and worship Him with everything we have and in every facet, stage, and age of our lives. Our obedience is what moves God; it's what causes Him not to hesitate in working all things concerning us in our favor.

It's not always necessary for us to know all the details of God's plan for us. If God revealed everything to us at once, we would find a way to insert ourselves into his plan, thinking that we could somehow add value to it when in fact, God's will and His way are perfect all by themselves. Rather than allowing ourselves to succumb to the anxiety that is so prevalent today about what may or may not happen to us, as Christians, we must hold fast to the biblical truths we have learned and take comfort and embrace the peace that comes from knowing God alone (Romans 5:1-5). No matter what our outcomes are, God will work all things for our good and His glory if we allow him to do the work and be Lord over our everything.

My Inspiration: God is able to take your life, with all of the headache, all of the pain, all of the regret, all of the missed opportunities and use you for His glory
~ Charles R. Swindoll

HEAVEN SPEAKS TO ME: Write about an adverse time in your life when you know beyond a doubt that God worked it out for your good. Explain how God was glorified in that situation.

_____
_____
_____
_____
_____
_____
_____
_____
_____
_____
_____
_____

Scripture Reading: Romans 5:1-5, Malachi 3:10, Genesis 50:20, Hebrews 13:5, 13:8, James 1:17

PRAYER: Precious Savior! You are my buckler. Thank you for shielding me from the devastation that could have fallen upon me. My life could be so much worst. But God! Help me not to complain about what I go through, but rather urge me by your spirit to walk in faith, knowing that for every adverse thing I experience, you are well able to work it out for my good. Amen!

Week Fourteen

Journey from Lo-Debar

◆◆◆◆◆◆◆◆◆◆

Jesus looked at them and said, "With man this is impossible, but with God all things are possible."

Matthew 19:26

Some time ago, I watched a show that documented a young girl's journey to finding members of her biological family. She had been adopted as a child by a well-off family but always felt that something was missing. She longed to know where she came from and to who she was connected. Though her adoptive parents were always truthful with her about the adoption, they feared her being rejected should she ever locate her real parents; yet, they vowed to help in any way they could. They began the search where it all started, hundreds of miles away from where they were. The father had moved from the state they were in because of his job, so naturally, they would go back to where the adoption took place as a starting point.

After searching for a few years, to their surprise, they received a lead that led them right to their community—only a few blocks away. This lead ended up being the encouragement they needed. The woman's biological brother lived a few blocks away! Their reunion was so heartfelt it brought tears to my eyes. The brother shared all of his struggles and how he was moved from one foster care to another but was never fortunate enough to have someone adopt him. The stories of abuse were heart-wrenching. He said he often felt alone and forgotten. Of course, he had become a young adult but still longed for a family to call his own. His sister's adoptive family took him in as their own and loved him just as they had his sister.

Unfortunately, all stories of adoption don't end this way. Often, the fairytale ending is just that, a fairytale. Many children who have either been abandoned by their parents or orphaned feel as though they have been forgotten, and no one cares. Going from one foster home to the next can be very hard on a child, especially if they are mistreated and only used to get a paycheck. These children are exposed to all manner of horrific experiences and are taunted with words that are dogmatic and spoken with disdain. But, as we see in the story of Mephibosheth, son of Jonathan, a close friend of King David, speaking the right words to and over someone can change the trajectory of their life.

When Jonathan and his father Saul were killed in fear, Mephibosheth's nurse fled with him, and in doing so, he fell and became crippled. In the ensuing years, he was identified as an outcast, a nobody living on the outskirts of town. He was no longer a king's grandson. All of his privileges had been stripped from him through no fault of his own. It was customary that when a new king took the throne, they would annihilate the entire bloodline of the previous king so that no family members could rise and say that they were due the throne.

However, David had promised his good friend Jonathan that he would show kindness to any remaining members of Saul's household. At the appointed time, David asked if there were anyone left in the house of Saul. When he found out about Mephibosheth, he sent for him. With trembling, Mephibosheth appeared before David, fearing for his very life. However, instead of being killed, David showed kindness and welcomed him into the palace to eat at the King's table. Mephibosheth was speechless. No one had ever shown this crippled outcast kindness, especially at this level.

He had become used to being ridiculed and shamed. It didn't matter that his grandfather was once the King. He was just another nobody from the slums, a leftover from a dynasty long gone. He had allowed the hateful words of others to mar how he saw himself—as a dead dog, which for a Jew was considered repulsive and nasty. He had become accustomed to the disdain of others and could not fathom seeing himself as anything more than the crippled has-been from Lo Debar with no future. But David saw him differently. He saw him as someone worthy to sit at his royal table—as someone worthy of reaping the benefits of being in the King's palace.

Though we are not to think more highly of ourselves than we ought, it is a wonderful and life-altering thing when the King thinks of you in such a way and holds you in high esteem. Talking about an ego booster! It raised both his esteem and dignity. There is an old cliché that says, "Sticks and stones may break my bones, but words will never hurt me." That is the biggest fallacy ever! Words do hurt! Words can be damaging and ruin a person's reputation, confidence, and life. Just one kind word, one gentle gesture, and one act of mercy, on the other hand, can make all the difference in someone's life. It can give a soul that's ready to throw in the towel hope for a brighter tomorrow. Speak words that uplift and restore dignity, not tear down and demoralize. Use words of acceptance and not rejection and words that restore to wholeness, not destroy to pieces.

No matter what slum or dark place you may be in right now, God knows exactly where you are. He is well able to bring you out of that darkness and despair into His marvelous light. Be reflective of your journey to the wealthy place God has placed you and where He has brought you from. Be willing to help someone else on their journey from Lo Debar to a place of wealth and prosperity. Speak life into someone today. Be the hand they need to rise from their slumber and be restored.

My Inspiration: *If people are doubting how far you can go, go so far that you can't hear them anymore.*
~ **Michelle Ruiz**

HEAVEN SPEAKS TO ME: Have you ever had someone speak a word of encouragement to you? How about a condemning word? How did it make you feel? How will you ensure that you speak only words that edify and uplift others?

_____

_____

_____

_____

_____

_____

_____

_____

_____

_____

_____

_____

_____

_____

Scripture Reading: Romans 5:1-5, Genesis 50:20, Hebrews 13:5, 13:8; Psalms 139:13-14

PRAYER: Kind God, make me speak words of life and healing and not words that tear down and insult my brothers and sisters in Christ. Help me to respond with kind and gentle words and with your love. Amen!

Week Fifteen

God Sees Me

...And she called the name of the LORD that spake unto her, Thou God seest me: for she said, Have I also here looked after him that seeth me?

Genesis 16:13

I can remember hearing someone describe a person by saying they were low to the ground, meaning that they were short. Back then, way, way back then, I was not only short but petite, so I was easy to overlook sometimes. It would anger me when someone tall or with a big hat would sit or stand in front of me because I was sure not to see whatever was in front of both of us, nor would I be seen.

In elementary school, I was in line at recess one day, and names were being called for kickball teams. I was pretty good at kicking the ball and could run pretty fast to bases. I was an asset—at least in kickball. People wanted me on their team. On this day, however, everyone else's name was called except mine. I wondered what the problem was because I was usually called for this game, at least. My immature mind made me believe that no one wanted to play with me. So, what did I do? I left and retreated to a corner all by myself because I thought I had been blacklisted, and all my friends had turned their backs on me.

In those moments, I felt afraid of not having a friend to play with, lonely, and unwanted. Well, turns out I wasn't overlooked after all. I was just not seen! My teacher, the beautiful Ms. Smith—I just loved her so— happened to turn around and saw me alone, looking rather bewildered. She rushed over to see if I was alright and asked where I had been. I told her I had been there all along, but I wasn't picked. She apologized profusely and said she didn't even see me in line because the taller kids had blocked her view of me. I was immediately put in the game, and suddenly, life was good again.

How often have we been in situations where we felt like no one saw us? We wanted to play. We wanted to be put in the game. The game of life. Our circumstances made us afraid. Fearfulness crippled us and prevented us from wanting to move forward. Feelings of loneliness overshadowed any hope of being loved or maybe even just liked. We were lost with no compass to show us the way. But, God!

In the story of Hagar found in the book of Genesis, in the sixteenth chapter, we learn of a woman who was forced into an act that she did not want to engage in by her mistress, Sarai. She was mistreated and used for someone else's gain. Here was a woman who felt she had no choice but to obey because she was no more than a slave with no rights or opinions of her own. She was not able to tell anyone because no one would understand why she had to sleep with her mistress's husband against her will. She was in total desperation and with no clear direction, in pain, defenseless, without shelter or sustenance, and what's worst, she was pregnant! In her despair, she probably wondered whether anyone even cared about her and what she was going through.

If you find yourself in desperate straits and you are wondering the same as Hagar when she was alone at a well in the middle of the desert, then you can relate. Perhaps you have even wondered if God himself cared. You've been praying and praying and fasting and seeking, and things look to only get worst. Well, the answer to your questions is yes, He does care! Not only does he care, He sees. He sees your struggles. He knows your pain. He feels your hurt. God sees YOU!

How do you know? Because He's **El Roi**, the God that Sees. Not only does He see you, He sees the circumstances surrounding you and is waiting to make His presence known. He knows you, too. He knows your name and the number of strands of hair on your head (Matthew 10:30). You are the apple of His eye (Deut. 32:10). And you are fearfully and wonderfully made (Psalm 139:14).

So, the next time the enemy wants to remind you of the situation you're in and the failures you've had, boldly remind him who you are. That you are not God's plan B or C. You are His plan A. You are not an afterthought. He made you in His image and created a masterpiece in you. God sees you, and His unfailing love for you makes Him choose to see you as He created you to be, not as you are. Just think, if God only saw us as we are, in our sinful, broken states, His wrath would be kindled against us, and we would have to experience his judgment. So, do like Hagar and acknowledge the God that sees all. Give Him the praise and glory that He so rightfully deserves; then, sit back and watch Him move on your behalf.

My Inspiration: The struggle you're in today is developing the strength you need for tomorrow
~ **Author Unknown**

HEAVEN SPEAKS TO ME: *Have you ever been overlooked for anything? How did that make you feel? How did you react? What lessons have you learned since then?*

_____
_____
_____
_____
_____
_____
_____
_____
_____
_____
_____
_____
_____
_____
_____
_____

Scripture Reading: Isaiah 43:1-4, Psalm 8:4; Jeremiah 11:11; 1 Samuel 16:7; Hebrew 4:13

PRAYER: El Roi! Thank you for seeing me right where I am. Father, your all-seeing eyes are on the righteous, always watching over us during every season of our lives. Let my eyes and heart remain open to what you are doing on the earth and in me. Amen!

Week Sixteen

The Valley Low

◆◆◆◆◆◆◆◆◆◆◆

God is our refuge and strength, an ever-present Help in times of trouble.

Psalm 46:1

Years ago, when the western Big Valley was on the air, I loved watching the Barkleys. The character of Victoria Barkley, played by the beautiful Barbara Stanwyck, was that of a strong, courageous woman who was in no way timid. She had a fight in her that said loudly she was no pushover by any means. She stood tall and tough, always displaying as much grit as her sons, Heath and Nick. The writers of Big Valley were once asked why Nick always wore gloves, and the answer was that he never knew when he was going to have to punch somebody out, and the gloves prevented split knuckles. In other words, he was always ready should adversity dare to present itself.

In one particular episode, the sons had gone on a journey, and on the return trip home, they came to a valley that was surrounded by high mountains and big boulders graced with many clefts, which provided hiding places for the enemy to attack and catch them by surprise. As they rode along on their horses, deep in conversation and laughter, unbeknownst to them, there was a gang of bandits awaiting their arrival. Nick's gloves were not going to help him in this fight.

Unfortunately for him, he wasn't able to throw his gloves at the bandits, and suddenly they would fall from the blow. No, he needed something greater. Something far more powerful with the ability to travel at a fast speed and hit the target with force. Without it, they would surely die in the valley. Well, as the story goes, because it's the television and the good guys, or at least the stars of the show, always seem to come out on top, they somehow prevailed.

Wouldn't we love it if that was always the reality in real life? How many times in our lives have we found ourselves surrounded? We were just moseying along in life, looking neither to the right nor left, just simply doing life as we know it to be lived. Without warning, we are sideswiped by life's brutal wind and find ourselves thrown out of kilter right into the valley low. We get up and dust off like nothing ever happened, but we quickly find that there is still some residue of our valley experience screeching every time we take a step forward in faith.

Oftentimes, this is where the enemy comes to discourage us by parading our past mistakes, failures, and hurts in front of us, constantly reminding us of our valley lows. But, thanks be to God who always causes us to triumph (2 Cor. 2:14)! Even when the enemy thinks he has us cornered with nowhere to run or hide, Psalm 46 reminds us that God is our refuge and our strength and is an ever-present help in our time of need. We must remain mindful of the fact the events that took place in our valley season are just experiences and not our final destination!

Many of us do not like valley low experiences, but we all must go through them nonetheless. They are designed not only for our shaking but for our making as well. Though they make us want to run for cover, there is no provision for when we run—we must go through the process. God's provision comes from staying the course and fighting until the manifestation of our breakthrough comes to fruition. We can't run from the enemy in fear. If we start running, we will be running all our lives. If you have never learned to fight, the valley is a great starting place. We can learn a lot about ourselves and about God in the valley—even how to fight and win!

The valley can be a very lonely place, especially when all you can do is look up and see everyone else rejoicing on the mountaintop. Our promised land is manifested through the adversity of our valley low experiences. The place of our discomfort is the place of provision. Like God provided Abraham a ram in the bush, so will he provide for you in the valley. If we trust Him in the valley low, He will most assuredly continue to take care of us on the mountaintop.

My Inspiration: One sees great things from the valley; only small things from the peak.
~ Gilbert K. Chesterton

HEAVEN SPEAKS TO ME: Think of a time when you went through a valley low experience. How did that experience change you? In what ways does knowing what God says about valley lows change your viewpoint?

_____
_____
_____
_____
_____
_____
_____
_____
_____
_____
_____
_____
_____
_____
_____

Scripture Reading: Psalm 23:4; Isaiah 59:19, 2 Corinthians 2:14, Psalms 46

PRAYER: Great defender, thank you for lifting a standard against my enemies when they come in like a flood. May I live a reflective life so that I am always in remembrance of your protection and that you are indeed my refuge and my hiding place when I need You the most. Amen!

Week Seventeen

As a Man Thinketh

Casting down imaginations, and every high thing that exalteth itself against the knowledge of God, and bringing into captivity every thought to the obedience of Christ.

2 Corinthians 10:5

As a child, I remember the story of The Little Engine that Could by Watty Piper. It detailed the efforts of a train filled with toys and gifts for little boys and girls that, unfortunately, broke down before it reached the eager recipients. The train tried to enlist the assistance of several larger trains passing by, but only one, a blue train and little just like him, agreed to help him as they struggled to get over the hill, repeating the words "I think I can, I think I can" finally got them over.

The premise of this children's tale is positive thinking and a growth mindset. It's often used to teach young children to think positively, not just of themselves but of life as a whole. It illustrates believing in oneself, positive self-talk, and perseverance in a way that a child can understand and relate to. Tillie, the little engine, had a very kind, sweet, and enthusiastic personality. However, when it was time to "put her foot to the metal," she became persistent, fearless, brave, and confident. Why? Because she was dependable and she knew some expectant little people were waiting for what she had to deliver.

Though you may think this childhood favorite is rather juvenile, its great message still holds true today, even for us grown-ups. The way we see ourselves is the way people tend to treat us. Somehow, without even telling them, people can see confidence, courage, and strength. But, they can also see our timidity which in some cases has to do with how we view ourselves and what we believe about ourselves.

Author James Allen wrote a self-help book called As a Man Thinketh. In his discourse, he states that the key to understanding our lives is our ability to harness the power of our thought life, which in turn enables us to emulate the demeanor and attitude of positive and successful people. When I was growing up, my pastor used to say, "Your attitude controls your altitude." If you say you are successful, then you are. Likewise, if you say you are a failure, well, you know . . . as a man thinketh.

As Christians, we are familiar with positive thinking. Throughout both the old and new testaments of the bible, we are told to guard our minds (Proverbs 4:23), to change our mindset (Mark 9:23), and to have our minds renewed (Romans 12:2). The apostle Paul urges us in Philippians 2:5-11 to "Let this mind be in you that is also in Christ Jesus." If we have the mind of Christ, this means we do not allow the enemy to whisper negativity in our ears and allow it to go unchallenged but refute it with the Word of God that we know. Notice that I said, "the Word of God that we know." If we don't read the Word and permit God to engraft it in our hearts, then we have nothing to challenge the enemy with. We will end up believing all the untruths that he tells us.

Ponder this thought. If you bought a house full of new carpets and then someone came to your door with a wheel barrel of manure, would you invite them in and permit them to dump on your new carpet? Of course not! Though manure has its purpose, it has no business in our thought life. Failing to challenge the enemy and not taking your thoughts captive is like allowing him to just freely dump all his lies and negativity in our minds. Unfortunately, some people do just that. No wonder their lifestyles stink! Stop the stinking thinking. Stop selling your mental real estate to the enemy. Allow God to come and foreclose on the enemy's plan to misuse and abuse your mind. Regain control over your thought life. Renew your mind through regularly studying the Word of God. We gain strength, peace, confidence, and direction when we do so. We must permit ourselves to only think about what is true, lovely, honest, pure, just, and of a good report (Philippians 4:8). Right thinking will lead to us reaching greater altitudes in every area of our lives.

My Inspiration: There are no limits to what you can accomplish, except the limits you place on your own thinking.
~ **Brian Tracy**

HEAVEN SPEAKS TO ME: Are you a thinker that tends to overthink situations? In what ways have you allowed your negative thoughts to keep you from being who God has called you to be or pursuing what God wants you to pursue? What impact has those negative thoughts had on your spiritual walk and your ability to hear God?

_____
_____
_____
_____
_____
_____
_____
_____
_____
_____
_____
_____
_____
_____

Scripture Reading: Philippians 4:8, Romans 1:18-23, Philippians 2:6-11; Proverbs 4:23

PRAYER: Jesus, I thank you for being a mind regulator. I am grateful for a renewed mind that allows me to set my affections on things above and not on this earth and that allows me to see and think of myself as you have created me to be. Amen!

Week Eighteen

The Sameness of God

Jesus Christ the same yesterday, and today, and forever.

Hebrews 13:8

You don't hear much about Cream of Wheat anymore, but when I was a kid, we ate it what seemed like every day of the week. Money was extremely tight back then, and Mother was raising six kids by herself and working double shifts at Children's Hospital Los Angeles to make ends meet. But, despite my childish feelings about it, it was a wholesome meal on a budget. On some days, I would think, "Cream of Wheat again?" as if that would somehow change the reality of it all. Nevertheless, most mornings, it was the same. Despite my mother's efforts to instill gratitude and graciousness in me at a young age, my immaturity didn't permit me to see just how blessed we were to have that meager meal and a roof over our heads. When I reminisce on those days, I now realize just how fortunate we were and that we had a lot more than most kids I went to school with.

Throughout our lives, there are a whole lot of things that will change. People will come and go, and those that stay, well, they will just become different. Not necessarily in a bad way, but the kind of different that is inevitable with age and the changing of wants due to living past the age of 30 and just experiencing life. However, there are some things that you wish could stay the same, like our kids before they grow up and start to rebel. But the truth of the matter is, regardless of how much we want things to remain the same, they just simply don't. What we have, though, instead of the "sameness" we wish we could somehow take captive and freeze in time, are the memories that will, we hope, live on forever.

With everything around us changing, life can become so uncertain, with nothing being guaranteed. Yet somehow, that's not how our creator is. The sum of God's immutability encompasses all of his wonderful attributes. He is immutably powerful, gracious, merciful, and wise. In other words, the strength of His power never diminishes. His grace is always sufficient. His mercies are endless and new every morning. And his wisdom is infinite. He is the same God yesterday, today, and forever! He cannot and does not change. He is perfect in all His ways. Because He is Deity, a supernatural being, He is also all-knowing and omnipresent, so He is well aware of what concerns you. Why? Because your concerns are not the first concerns He has had to address. Just like many of the problems we face are the same, so is the only one who can solve them. The same God who delivered from the abusive relationship 20 years ago is the same God who will bring complete healing to an ailing body, despite the diagnosis, today. If He did it back then, He can do it again and again.

When life starts to feel mundane and redundant and it appears that you are stuck in a rut and unfulfilled, you can still find contentment and satisfaction in the sameness of God's grace and mercy. God's faithful provision when we have more months than money causes us to trust and depend on His care each day. Unlike many of our earthly friends, He is not a fair-weather friend. He is and always will be the one constant in our lives if we allow Him to be. We can always count on God.

My Inspiration: There is a sameness within us all. This sameness is the expression of God. When truth is expressed through love, the sameness in all of us awakens, the fog of forgetfulness is lifted and our spirits shine.
~ James Blanchard Cisneros

HEAVEN SPEAKS TO ME: How does coming to the realization that people tend to be anxious in situations when they forget what God has already done for them change how you respond to adversity? Write about a time when you had to be reminded of this and how it changed your perspective.

_____
_____
_____
_____
_____
_____
_____
_____
_____
_____
_____
_____
_____

Scripture Reading: Malachi 3:6; Numbers 23:19; 1 Timothy 1:17; James 1:17; John 1:2

PRAYER: God, you are the one true constant in my life. Thank you for being a God that I can rely on each time I need you. Help me to always trust in your faithfulness towards me and my loved ones. Don't let me waiver with the high tides of life. Let me always be reminded of your sameness. You were God back then, and you are God forevermore. Amen!

Week Nineteen

The Blessing of Brokenness

◆◆◆◆◆◆◆◆◆◆

The LORD is nigh unto them that are of a broken heart; And saveth such as be of a contrite spirit.

Psalm 34:18-20

As I pondered the title of this particular devotion, admittedly, I was reluctant because the words blessing and brokenness appear to be an oxymoron. How can being broken possibly be a blessing? Well, I suppose it's all about perspective—God's perspective, that is. I, like everyone else, do not like the pain, suffering, or feeling of being broken. The most difficult times in my life have been those times when I felt like I was broken, like nothing in my life worked. I felt as if I were a big mistake and wondered why I was even still here. It was a season of confusion. I thought I had done everything right, and yet life for me was far from blissful. I thought I was being punished by God when, in fact, He was trying to reposition me for a breakthrough.

I was recently reminded of a book by the same name by Dr. Charles Stanley. One of the points he brought to light about brokenness stuck with me. He wrote that our willingness to be broken by God has everything to do with our relinquishing control over our lives as if we ever had control at all. The illusion that we have created of our having control over anything in our lives is what God wants to dismantle. We live in a time when there is much emphasis on success, wealth, happiness, and prosperity. The last thing we want to think about is being broken.

Society has conditioned us to believe that if we have money and material things, life is good. But, as we listen to the news, we find that money is not everything. We tend to be quick to praise when we have money in our pockets but can't always seem to muster up the strength when things are tight. Praise without repentance is a moot point to God. There are many people with a lot of money but who are far from God because they refuse to refrain from allowing their possessions to be to them what God should be—their sole source and not just one of them.

The Psalmist tells us that the LORD is near to those who are of a broken heart and saves those with a contrite spirit. No one has to tell us that we are repeat offenders; we know when we do things that are contrary to the word. But, it's those who do not let their sins go without being repented for and whose heart is truly broken over the things that break God's heart. Those are the ones that the Lord is nearest to, not the ones with the largest bank accounts. Now, that is not to say that you can't have wealth and still have a rooted and grounded relationship with God through his word and prayer. Unfortunately, though, we see so often the love of money being the root of all evil (1 Timothy 6:10) instead of it being used to bless others.

We need to understand the reasons why we must be broken. God only wants to break us so that He can remake us. He wants to make us better, not bitter. A state of brokenness is the only way we can truly experience God. He begins the process by stripping us of our self-sufficiency and dependency on any other thing or person besides himself. Perhaps you've already experienced circumstances so shattering you may be wondering whether it's even possible to pick up the pieces. And maybe you can't. But God certainly can—and the good news is, He will. He will reassemble the tiny shreds of your life into a wholeness that only the broken can know and appreciate. Being able to feel joy again after a long period of mourning can be euphoric. God can send a blessing right in the middle of your brokenness, but only when you release the reins and allow Him to take full charge of your life. Brokenness is not a death sentence but rather a new lease on a wonderfully rewarding life in Jesus Christ.

My Inspiration: "Never be ashamed about being broken, because strength is nothing but pain that's been repaired."
~ **Trent Shelton**

HEAVEN SPEAKS TO ME: Have you ever felt broken, like Humpty Dumpty, who fell off the wall and couldn't be put back together again? Write about how hearing, learning, and understanding God's word helped you to see your brokenness through a new set of lenses instead of viewing it as a punishment from God.

_____
_____
_____
_____
_____
_____
_____
_____
_____
_____
_____
_____
_____
_____

Scripture Reading: Psalm 51:17-19, Psalm 34:18-20, 2 Corinthians 7:10; Psalm 147:3; 1 Peter 5:10

PRAYER: Thank you, Father God, for loving me enough to break me but not destroy me. Help me to see my brokenness as an opportunity for You to remake me into the person You created me to be. Thank you for sculpturing and molding me for Your great use. Amen!

<u>Week Twenty</u>

As-Is Purchased

*All that the Father giveth me shall come to me; And him
that cometh to me I will in no wise cast out.*

John 6:37

Shopping with my mother was always a treat. If one of her stops was a boring visit to the fabric store, those that endured the trip were sure to be treated to a tasty lunch and perhaps even walk away with a bag or two of their own. However, when those trips included going to the Goodwill or Salvation Army, I made it my business to be MIA. I was not a Goodwill kinda kid. In fact, during that time, I thought it was downright embarrassing to have to shop there. All I thought they sold was old, raggedy hand-me-down items that no one else wanted and that people of any decent reputation would never step foot in a store like that, and I wasn't about to be the laughing stock of the schoolyard if anyone found out.

    This all changed when one day, my mother took me with her to the Goodwill. I was tricked and bamboozled into going, so I didn't have a very good attitude about going inside, but she reprimanded me and made me go in anyway. I was instructed to "touch nothing and ask for nothing." Lucky for me, we were not there to shop for clothes, and I had absolutely no interest in anything else. My mother sewed a lot. I can remember many days coming home from school on her days off from the hospital to scrap pieces of material, cut off strings of thread and pattern paper that my siblings and I would have to clean up.

That day in the Goodwill store, my mother was looking for a certain kind of teapot. She had several beautiful ones she kept on display in the china cabinet in the dining room. She would find the most beautiful teapots and cups and make baskets she called "Tea for Two" and sell them. People would purchase these baskets from her to give as gifts and as a treat to themselves. She would put all kinds of teas and cinnamon sticks and whatever else she thought was relevant, depending on who was making the purchase. She was so gifted at making things beautiful.

I was amazed at the treasures we found that day, some still with the original tags. But, some tags read, "sold as-is." Those were the items that were slightly damaged but could probably still be used if the right person bought them and knew how to make them whole again. Needless to say, my perspective of Goodwill changed that day. I guess you could say I started to have a more open mind about it. Of course, I could never admit it back then, but I enjoyed not only the time spent with Mother but also rummaging through all the merchandise. Every so often, we would find something worth looking at.

When I think about that day in the Goodwill store, I think about the great sacrifice that Jesus gave on our behalf, the ultimate gift of his shed blood on that old rugged cross on a hill called Calvary. I've heard preachers speak on how Jesus could have called ten thousand angels to rescue him, but He, who knew no sin, hung there becoming sin so that the debt of our trespasses could be paid.

As Jesus hung on the cross, the Father gave him a glimpse of the potential he placed inside of mankind—the potential to be salt and light to a fallen world. He knew He had the power to change, clean, and redeem us to do His good pleasure on the earth. So, Jesus gave His life for people who didn't deserve it based solely on the potential He knew the Father had placed within us. God knew He could make us like new again with the sacrifice of His only begotten son. He purchased us as-is! He bought our salvation. He paid the price. We couldn't earn it, and we surely couldn't afford to buy it—we could only accept it.

He didn't say to His Father, "Dad, I don't want to do this because these people are not right. They are damaged, dirty, and sinful with a lot of holes and stains on them." Instead, His love for us made Him look past all our faults to our needs. He knew we needed a savior. He knew that if He didn't pay our debt that we would have no hope of surviving the wrath of the Father. So, instead of seeing us as our sinful selves, He decided to look at us as the Father created us to be. He saw us as people worth dying for. He didn't wait until we were cleaned up and dressed in our Sunday best or until we earned our doctorate or bought our first home, or even reached the top of our socio-economic status. No, He did it while we were yet in our trespasses. He still decided to die.

When my mom and I returned home from our day of plunking, as she liked to call it, we unwrapped and admired our treasures. She ran some dishwater and gave what she had found a good cleaning. She had found what she was looking for, a beautiful teapot with two matching cups and saucers. Once cleaned, they were even more beautiful than originally thought to be. She had a keen eye for this sort of thing. Now, all those many years later, I still like to peek in the Goodwill store from time to time. I'm still keeping an open mind. I never know what I may find, even if I have to purchase as-is.

My Inspiration: Things work out best for those who make the most out of how things work out

~ **John Wooden**

HEAVEN SPEAKS TO ME: How does it make you feel to know that you are accepted by God just as you are? Those times in your life when you didn't feel accepted, how did it make you feel, and how did that experience help you to be more cognizant of how you accept others?

_____
_____
_____
_____
_____
_____
_____
_____
_____
_____
_____
_____
_____
_____

Scripture Reading: 1 Corinthians 6:19-20, Galatians 3:13-15, Colossians 1:14; Titus 2:14; Revelations 5:9

PRAYER: Perfect and kind God, thank you for loving and accepting me as-is. I am so grateful that I don't have to be perfect for you to love me and care for me. Your compassion is unprecedented, and I thank you for mending me in my broken places instead of discarding me. Amen!

Week Twenty-One

Cure for the Sin-Sick Heart

◆◆◆◆◆◆◆◆◆

If we confess our sins, he is faithful and just and will Forgive us our sins and purify us from all unrighteousness.

1 John 1:9

One year, I traveled back home to California to visit my siblings during my birthday month. It's always a good time being with my siblings as we reminisce about old times. This day one of my sisters recalled a time when I had gotten in trouble for having a bad attitude. I was brought up in front of everyone and told by the person who called me out that "they were the seasoning for my soup." In other words, they had the cure for my bad attitude, and they were going to give me what I deserved. After they got through with me, I was going to be cured for life, and my attitude would suddenly unveil its rebirth. Well, I guess it sounded good to them at the time. I, on the other hand, was seething with anger. How dare they call me out like that? I could see the smirks on the other youth's faces as they tried desperately to keep the laughs in. You literally could have sold me for a penny! I wanted to vanish into thin air. I was humiliated.

Though it wasn't very funny at the time, when I think of it now, it is rather humorous. Of course, no one says that anymore; at least, I have not heard it since that day, thankfully, but I can laugh about it now. For many of us, our memories of the cure-all were the switch that our disappointed mothers would make us go and pick out so we could receive our just reward of a reprimand for the wrong we had done. Mind you, it was all done in love, right? Well, try telling that to my backside because it wasn't buying it. Yet, we know that our actions have consequences that we are never too keen about having to suffer through.

We are fortunate that God has blessed us with the expertise of scientists and doctors working collectively to develop cures and vaccines for many of the infectious diseases we have been plagued with through the years. As history will show, the Bubonic plague of 1347 claimed millions of lives in Europe and surrounding areas. The Spanish Flu of 1918 killed approximately 50 million people. Then there was H1N1 and the Ebola outbreak. All of these diseases needed a cure. Scientists, the CDC, and WHO scrambled to find the right combination of compounds to secure a vaccination because people were afraid and fearful of losing their lives and the lives of their loved ones. Not to ever downplay the severity of these diseases, as the losses were astronomical, but there is certainly one disease far greater than all of these combined that you never hear about in the headlines of the Sunday newspaper or as a breaking news segment on CNN. You never hear about the deadly disease of a sinful heart. You never hear the heads of the CDC or the WHO speak about how they are scrambling for a cure for sin because it is running rampant and people are losing their lives, their minds, and their very souls. But, whether it's talked about or not, there is indeed a cure.

The cure that I speak of has no respect for persons. No one is excluded from receiving this vaccine. Every race and gender is invited: people of all stages and ages. Drunkards, drug addicts, prostitutes, and scoundrels are all welcome. This vaccine is so potent that it only takes a whiff, and you're cured! It is offered to all souls who are willing to surrender, submit and admit that they are out of resources, that all other measures have been taken, and all other avenues driven down have only led to dead-ends at every turn. Don't allow the enemy and the trouble of this world to cause you to flatline. Stretch out your hands and reach for your salvation. Jesus is standing with outstretched arms, waiting to snatch you right out of Satan's strong grip.

What qualifies Jesus to be your sin vaccine instead of the likes of Muhammed or maybe even the guy on the corner lot down the street, Mr. Jones? The answer is quite simple. Jesus was willing to and did die for you and me. He was sinless. I don't know about you, but I can't think of one other soul who would be willing, let alone do something of that magnitude for a person so undeserving. If you're wondering what you must do to be saved and receive this vaccination; this new lease on life, just put your trust in the Master! Confess your sins and allow Him to finish the good work He started in you. Internalize and ingest Him. Inject the Jesus vaccine and allow it to flow through your veins. Let Jesus be your sin vaccination today. When we repent, He throws our sins in the sea of forgetfulness and remembers them no more (Micah 7:19).

My Inspiration: God has two dwellings; one in heaven, and the other in a meek and thankful heart
~ Izaak Walton

HEAVEN SPEAKS TO ME: When you got your last flu shot did you sense a feeling of relief like you had an added layer of security against getting a bad winter cold? How does that feeling compare to when you confessed your sins and accepted Jesus into your heart?

_____

_____

_____

_____

_____

_____

_____

_____

_____

_____

_____

_____

Scripture Reading: Matthew 9:4-6, Psalm 55:21, Isaiah 1:5, Mark 7:20-23

PRAYER: Divine healer, my cure-all and be-all, You, oh Lord, are the reason I have life everlasting! My future is brighter now that I have been made new and my sins have been eradicated by Your Holy word and through the sacrifice Your son, Jesus made on the cross. Amen!

Week Twenty-Two

Lifeline

◆◆◆◆◆◆◆◆◆

Therefore, confess your sins to each other and pray for Each other so that you may be healed. The prayer of A righteous man is powerful and effective.

James 5:16

Some years back, I returned to live with my mother after being laid off after 11 years from my job at the newspaper. It was difficult having to go back after all those years of being on my own. However, it was good to partake of the good meals Mother always made. Her touch on any meal always made it so much better. One of the most memorable things, though, was her early morning prayers. She was so disciplined and committed to her prayer life. She faithfully arose each morning at the crack of dawn, around 5 or 5:30 am, sometimes earlier, to talk to her Father. I never saw my mother cry unless she was in worship or praying.

The only other time I saw Mother cry was after receiving the news of my older brother passing so unexpectedly. It was almost unbearable for her. The agony I saw, for the first time, in my mother's eyes as tears of unproportionate grief poured down her pained face was extremely difficult to watch. I loved my brother and missed him, but it was hard for me to grieve him because I was so concerned about Mother. She was so strong and full of faith. I just couldn't fathom the pain she was feeling having lost a child. I wouldn't wish that pain on my worst enemy. It seemed like she cried for the entire day.

But, on the day of my brother's celebration of life, there were no tears of sadness. I don't think I had ever seen my mother dance so hard. As I watched her dance in front of his casket, once again in awe, I was amazed at the strength she displayed. Her praise that day was so on purpose and focused. It was as if she had come to terms with him being gone and was comforted in knowing that he was with the Father, and that made it all alright.

Weeks later, I accepted a job at the American Red Cross in St. Louis, Missouri. I wanted to leave early as it was my first day of work, and since I had to commute across the mighty Mississippi River, I wanted to make a good impression. I lived in Illinois but worked and played a lot in Missouri. Mother's room was right by the staircase, and mine was down the hall, so I had to pass her room to go down the steps. Before heading down the steps, I stood at her door as I often did and listened while she prayed. I would hear her call out her children's names to God, asking for His blessings over our lives. That morning, however, I didn't hear my name called. I heard all the others but not mine. I stood there a while longer, thinking that she would get around to me, but she never did. As I slowly walked down the steps, I was crushed. I knew my day would not go well; at least, that's how I was feeling. I needed and depended on those prayers. How would I make it through my day or, better yet, my life without them? It was a gloomy day, and I felt lost.

I hadn't realized just how dependent I was on Mother's prayers until they were gone forever. God welcomed this great woman of God home a few years ago. It had to have been the saddest day of my life. I was once again lost. Who would pray for me now? Who would I call when I needed encouragement—a word to lift my spirits when I'm feeling down? God gave me the answer to those questions one day in my quiet time. He reminded me just how immature I was when it came to my prayer life. I had been riding on my mother's prayers all my life, and now it was time to develop my very own relationship. My very own lifeline. As I thought back over the years, I knew everything was not always peachy for us. Mother sometimes worked double shifts at the hospital to make ends meet, but I never heard her complain or shed one tear because of what we didn't have. She just prayed. It was her source of life. When her world was falling apart, no one ever knew it because her lifeline was always in motion. Prayer to the One who made all things well. The One who made all things work together for her good. The One who had made a way when there was no way. This is why she always came out on top and rarely went without. She was connected to her lifeline!

I am still learning to develop and connect to my lifeline through the power of prayer. In doing so, life has gotten much sweeter and much less frustrating. We can stand waist-deep in a gushing spring and still be dehydrated and perish of extreme thirst. It's not until you bend down and take a scoop in your hands and take a big gulp of the refreshing spring water and swallow that it becomes the lifeline needed for your nourishment and ultimate survival. Though we will have struggles, loss, and grief, coping will be much easier if you bend and cling to prayer. I encourage everyone reading this to make a lasting connection to the Lifeline. You'll be so glad you did.

My Inspiration: Prayer is aligning ourselves with the purposes of God.
— **E. Stanley Jones**

When Heaven Speaks

HEAVEN SPEAKS TO ME: Recall when you first learned about prayer. How has your prayer life evolved, or has it? If not, in what ways can you improve it so that it becomes a way of life and what you rely on to get you through the rough seasons? How can prayer be a catalyst for getting the answers you need?

_____
_____
_____
_____
_____
_____
_____
_____
_____
_____
_____
_____
_____
_____
_____

Scripture Reading: Philippians 4:6, Acts 2:21, Job 42:10, Psalm 102:17

PRAYER: Thank you, Father God, for being my lifeline when I need you most and for always extending a listening ear to my faintest cries. Lord, your invitation to come to you to all who are weary and heavy-laden gives me strength and hope to believe all things are possible through You. Amen!

Week Twenty-Three

BIG

Ah Lord GOD! Behold, thou hast made the heaven and the earth by thy great power and stretched out arm, and there is nothing too hard for thee.

Jeremiah 32:17

Kids are immature. It's in their nature to be that way; they can't help it. What we adults think is juvenile and sometimes comical behavior is, to them, major catastrophes. This was especially true as a second-grader. During recess at South Park Elementary School, where I grew up, my posse and I would often run to the gate and watch cars and fight over which ones were ours. The school was at the corner of Manchester and Avalon in south-central LA, so the streets were regularly busy with traffic. This particular day, I had chosen a big long rust color Cadillac. I think the problem was, so did Jacqueline. I still say I called it first, but she insisted that she did.

Even at my age, I knew in my heart that it was silly to get mad for real over such a minute thing, but I still obliged her in the spat. I told her she could have the red car instead, but she wasn't having it. She wanted mine. So Ms. Smith, our teacher, had to intervene. She rushed over to see what the commotion was all about. We explained what was happening, and she asked why one of us couldn't just take the other car. Turns out Jacqueline wanted my car because it was bigger. To our surprise, Ms. Smith chuckled loudly and said, "Just because something is bigger doesn't mean that it's better." Neither of us agreed with her because, in our young minds, bigger was absolutely better. Eventually, it was settled that we would share the ride, and since we were friends, we could go places together, which would make it even more fun to ride in. But then there was the argument, "Why do you always get to choose where we go?" It was never-ending.

Isn't that how we do even as adults? We can't fathom how someone else could be doing so much better than we are. As Christians, we see people in the world who are not even trying to live a Godly lifestyle, and yet they seem to be prospering—living large with all the bigger and better things we desire. We often think or, at best, wonder if it's really greener on the other side. Our curiosity gets the best of us, and we sometimes go to the other side in search of what's bigger and better, only to find that what God had already provided was all and what we needed all along.

Throughout scripture, we read how God will supply all our needs (Philippians 4:19), that He owns the cattle on a thousand hills (Psalm 50:10), and He will withhold no good thing from them that walk uprightly (Psalm 84:11). Yet, we tend to underestimate God's ability to heal, sustain and provide for us in our times of need. He is way too big to be put in the small boxes we create because we lack the faith to believe for the bigger and better things He has in store for those who trust and believe that His word is indeed true.

He is bigger than all our problems. Bigger than every sickness and disease. He is bigger than our greatest fears and the giants we have to face. He is bigger than every mountain that stands in our way. He has even given us the power to speak to the mountains and tell them to get out of our way (Mark 11:23). He is bigger than the lust of our flesh and the sexual desires that so often tempt and entangle us. He is bigger than any amount of debt that we can ever owe. He's more vast than all the oceans combined and the heavens above. He is Indescribable!

For this, we ought to forever stand in awe of Him, who created the universe and made everything on the earth. Why not serve a Big God like that? Why not trust a God that can do anything but fail or lie? He is, without a doubt, the master inventor and sculptor who continues to intricately craft each of us into who He wants us to be. Yes, it is You, oh Lord, who is the giver of the greatest concepts and ideas. Ever been given a God idea? I have. You're reading it right now. You do exceedingly above all we could ever ask or think. Lord, you are Big!

My Inspiration: God always has something for you, a key for every problem, a light for every shadow, a relief for every sorrow, and a plan for every tomorrow.
~ **Unknown**

HEAVEN SPEAKS TO ME: Just how BIG is God to you? Name a time when God showed up in your situation in a big way. How did His mere presence make your issue shrink down to size and submit to His will?

_____

_____

_____

_____

_____

_____

_____

_____

_____

_____

_____

_____

_____

Scripture Reading: Isaiah 55:8-9, Job 26:14, Jeremiah 23:23-24, Psalm 139:7-12

PRAYER: Omnipotent, omniscient, and omnipresent God. I am so glad you are so much BIGGER than all my problems and circumstances. God, I thank you for your sovereignty in my life. Your loud presence has made all the difference. Help me never minimize you to fit in my finite world. Amen!

Week Twenty-Four

Bold Enough to Ask

...."Give me a blessing; since you have given me land in the Negev, give me also springs of water." So he gave her the upper springs and the lower springs.

Joshua 15:19

Have you ever wanted to ask a question but were afraid to because you feared the response? I have, both as a child and as an adult. Instead of just coming right out with it, I'd make small talk or hint around at what I wanted or maybe even jokingly ask with the hope that I'd be taken seriously. The problem with "beating around the bush," so to speak, is that you run the risk of not only wasting precious time by talking about unimportant and unnecessary things but you are also delaying a response that just might be in your favor.

We are all familiar with the passage of scripture that says, "Ask and it shall be given," right? Well, depending on what and how you ask some folks depends on whether or not you will be given it. Wouldn't it be nice if we could all just simply ask for whatever we wanted from whomever we wanted it, and without any exchange of words or hesitation, it would be given to us? Of course, we would then have to be responsible for having and maintaining those possessions. I heard a story once of someone who had gone on a game show and won big. They won a car, a trip, and several other items. It was all great at first. However, the overjoyed winner didn't realize that they would be responsible for all the taxes on it all. Soon after, it wasn't all smiles anymore. After all, they had to sell most of what was won because they couldn't afford to pay the taxes.

I am thankful that I can go to my heavenly Father and ask for whatever I want that aligns with his will for me, and He will give it to me. He won't send the tax collector or some guy named Big Tiny after me two weeks later, telling me to pay up or else. Like any good Father, He willingly and freely gives to His children, and in some cases, he gives us more than what we asked for, the overflow. This was the case with Achsah, the daughter of Caleb. We read about her in Joshua 15 when, after she had just been married, she persuaded her new husband to ask Caleb for a field of land. But, when they got to Caleb, in excitement, Achsah leaped off her donkey and ran to her father, and out came the request. "Give me a blessing: for thou hast given me a south land; give me also springs of water."

Caleb was a good father. He had already given his daughter and her new husband land. However, the land he gave was on an arid southern plain with no water supply. She was a virtuous woman, one who was observant and forward-thinking. She had only been married a very short while and had already surveyed the land and realized they needed water. She also knew that without a proper water supply, her land would have no vegetation, and no kind of agricultural endeavor would be able to thrive.

Now some people would have been afraid to ask for more, but she was bold and courageous. She was on a mission to ensure her new family had what they needed, and she could not afford to be shy about it, nor did she have time for idle chit-chat. When she arrived, she got right down to business. Because she was not too proud to ask for more, not only did she receive the upper spring, but he gave her the lower springs as well, which would ensure the productivity and flourishment of her newly acquired land. Her confidence in asking enabled her to return home with a sense of security that her household would indeed be fed, their earnings potential would skyrocket, and their net worth would go through the roof—all because she had the nerve to ask for more.

Whatever your need is today, do not be afraid to go to your heavenly Father and ask. Ask boldly, courageously, and without hesitation for what you will, knowing and believing that He will give you the desires of your heart if you delight in Him and that whatever you ask for in His holy name, it shall be given to you. So go ahead and ask for something more. Something big!

My Inspiration: "If we did all the things we are capable of, we would literally astound ourselves."
Thomas A. Edison

HEAVEN SPEAKS TO ME: Have you always been bold? Explain a time when you didn't feel bold, but you knew God was calling you to something bigger that required you to step out in confidence. Write about the moment God gave you the boldness to say and or do what you know he was asking of you. How did that accomplishment make you feel?

_____
_____
_____
_____
_____
_____
_____
_____
_____
_____
_____
_____
_____

Scripture Reading: Joshua 15:13-19, 1 John 5:13-15, James 4:2-3; 2 Corinthians 3:12

PRAYER: Lord, you did not give me the spirit of fear but of power, love, and soundness of mind. Thank you for empowering me to do what you are calling me to do. May I always rely on your strength and might to carry out your plans in my life. Amen!

Week Twenty-Five

Brutal Distractions

I am saying this for your own good, not to restrict you, but that you may live in a right way in undivided devotion to the Lord.

1 Corinthians 7:35

When trying to focus and give our undivided attention to something or someone, distractions can be quite a nuisance. They seem to come at the most inopportune time and throw us out of kilter. Not only that, distractions can have adverse effects and sometimes be fatal.

I must have been about 10 or 11 years old when I was forced to eat only soft, mushy foods for about two weeks. These soft foods included mashed potatoes and Cream of Wheat cereal mostly. The cause was a combination of my being a little distracted and probably a whole lot of hard-headedness.

A friend and I had been out playing hard that day. She lived around the corner and down the block. Now I was told that I could play out front of the apartments we lived in but not go down the street and around the corner. Well, being myself, I decided to ease on down the road anyway. Unfortunately, the playtime got good, I lost track of time, and it was getting dark. To get home quicker, my friend and I decided to race back to my place. Now, this wasn't just a race; that would have been too much like right, and we were not right, at least not that day. We decided to challenge ourselves and see who could get there first. With our eyes closed. Well, when I got to Mr. Duffy's house on the corner, I heard my friend yell something, and

I turned to look back but never stopped moving. As I turned back around, it was just in time to run fast-paced, face-first right dead into Mr. Duffy's long black Cadillac. Thankfully, it was parked but I hit my mouth so hard that it swelled up like a duck's beak. I couldn't eat for days all because I was hard-headed, I mean, distracted.

Distractions can come at us in all forms and from all directions, but the outcome of a distraction is usually the same: we lose focus and get off track. Sometimes, they are subtle and sneak upon us. They catch us by surprise. Sometimes, they may even come at a very high price. No matter how your distractions come, they all have three purposes; to deter us from experiencing what God has for us, take us out of our position to receive what God wants to give us, or keep us from knowing our true identity in Christ. Once we have allowed the enemy to challenge our identity in Christ, he will then try to convince us that we are not who we say and believe we are in Christ. When we can identify our distractions and take them before a merciful God, He is well able to get us back on course and in His perfect will.

The word *distraction* comes from the Latin word dis̄, "apart," and trahere, "drag." In other words, distractions drag or lure us away from our current tasks. Depending on how distracted we allow ourselves to become and for how long, getting back on track can be a challenge but not impossible. Refocusing spiritually after being distracted isn't difficult at all, but it certainly requires us to be purposeful and intentional about where we devote our time and what we give our attention to. If we are not careful, our distractions can come at such a high price and have such brutal consequences that we either do not want to or cannot afford to pay.

Luring us away from our God-given task is not all distractions can do. They affect our response time and can cause us to lose the ground we've gained in our spiritual walk. When God sends a word and gives us instructions to move or go, and our attention is directed elsewhere, we will be Johnny-Come-Lately to what God is calling us to do and where He has told us to be. There are great repercussions for being in the wrong place at the wrong time doing the wrong thing. Let us keep looking to the hills where we know our help comes from. Destiny is waiting. Don't be distracted. Keep our eyes fixed on Jesus and let nothing the enemy dangles in front of us cause there to be a turning away from God.

My Inspiration: Say NO to distractions so you can say YES to your destiny.
~ **Thema Davis**

HEAVEN SPEAKS TO ME: How do you handle distractions? Do you allow them to take you off course? In what ways are you learning to stay focused on the things God has called you to? In what ways has being distracted cost you?

_____
_____
_____
_____
_____
_____
_____
_____
_____
_____
_____
_____
_____
_____

Scripture Reading: 1 Peter 5:8, James 1:21-25, 1 Corinthians 10:13; Titus 3:3-7; Colossians 2:13-15

PRAYER: God, this world is filled with all manner of distractions and alluring things. Father, help me keep my focus on you at all times lest I stray. For every assignment you give me, let me complete it in a way that pleases you. Amen!

Week Twenty-Six

Love's Magnitude

*The Lord your God in your midst, The Mighty One, Will save;
He will rejoice over you with gladness, He
Will quiet you with His love, He will rejoice over you with singing.*

Zephaniah 3:17

I love music and movies. In fact, I'm not sure which I love more. Well, maybe music. That's in my blood. I can't help it. Anyway, the soulful Al Green sang a song called *Love and Happiness*. Part of the lyrics says, "Love will make you do wrong," then it goes on to say, "Love will also make you do right." That's a good oldie, but a goodie that will make you go, heeeyy! With fingers popping and all . . . but, I digress. This is a devotional. Ahem, okay, I'm back.

There's also a movie, *Boomerang*, starring comedian Eddie Murphy and Halle Berry. In the movie, there is an oft-repeated line in which Ms. Berry yells at Mr. Murphy when she says in a very matter-of-fact way, "Love would have brought you home last night," as he so sadly tries to explain his bad behavior and MIA status to her.

Love is a very powerful emotion. As the song says, it can make us do a lot of things that, had we not experienced it, we would probably have never done. Yet, the absence of love can have the same adverse effect on those who refuse to give and or accept it. We have all heard about the love book in the bible. We've grown up hearing 1 Corinthians 13, both read and exegetical sermons given. Most of us should know it verbatim by now. In this passage, Paul gave us a great example of what true love is and what it looks like lived out. Yet, we tend to form our own opinions and create definitions of love in ways that look nothing like what scripture describes. We often take it for granted when given it. Some desire it but simply don't know how to receive it. Others reject it outright because they've never experienced it.

The love that we read about in scripture is life-changing. When we really know and fully understand who created love and why it even exists, loving our neighbors will become so much easier, even when it's not reciprocated. Our Father in heaven loved us so much he was willing to look beyond all our faults; they were (are) many, and saw what we were truly in need of. You've seen babies cry, right? Well, most of the time, they are not just doing so for the fun of it. They are crying because there is something else going on that is making them uncomfortable, and in their infant state, that is the only way they can get someone to pay attention to their issue.

Likewise, God knows the real root cause of our behavior. His love makes him slow to anger, patient, and long-suffering. He is not short on love, as it is His great love for us that caused Him to send His only begotten son to die for our sins. It was Jesus' love that made him deem us worth dying for.

No matter how you define love, know that our creator's magnitude of love is more than we can ever comprehend. He is love! He invented it. We only know what love is and what it should feel like because of Him. His love is great enough to pull us out of our lonely, depressing places. Those places we find ourselves in when the enemy and his minions are dispatched to make us feel like giving up. Like we don't have any business being blessed and thriving in our wealthy places—our places of wholeness and plenty. His love covers a multitude of sins, guilt, and shame. His love heals! Open your heart to heaven's magnitude of love. When you do, you will never be the same.

My Inspiration: Whoever loves much, performs much and can accomplish much, and what is done in love is done well
~ **Vincent Van Gogh**

HEAVEN SPEAKS TO ME: Have you felt the magnitude of God's unfailing love lately? Explain how that made you feel. In what ways do you make concerted efforts to express God's love in how you treat others and in how you share the love of God with unbelievers?

_____
_____
_____
_____
_____
_____
_____
_____
_____
_____
_____
_____

Scripture Reading: Joshua 15:13-19, 1 John 5:13-15, James 4:2-3; Ephesians 3:18; Romans 8:28-38

PRAYER: Lord God, your love for me is unprecedented. No other love have I known that is so great. Thank you for not waiting until I got perfect to love me; you love and accept me just as I am. Amazing is your unfailing and never-ending love for me. Amen

INTERLUDE

Triumphant Me

The Spoken WORD

By Tize Symplrix Williams

Dim, dark, barren-I couldn't see an exit
In an endless cycle of circles, I seemed to be destined
Each round seemed to be deeper than the last;
hopes of a peaceful present
had become a dream of the past
Fading fast was the faith I once held on to
Saving Grace was the thing that needed to be renewed
WHERE-IS-MY-RESCUE!!??
Oh, my God, do you hear me calling out to you?
Please send your peace and make these cycles end.
Silence my mind. Let your healing begin.
Come destroy the doubt that plagues my weary soul
While I'm stuck and broken, please, my Lord, help me yield COMPLETE control.
My own strength is gone-I have none left

THIS is the lowest I have EVER felt
My heart is shattered-ripped to the core
But-with this next breath-I cry out to You once more!!

In that exact moment, a crack entered into my mind's door.
I sensed the heaviness of His presence upon me for sure
I began to cry and cry some more.
I began to travail like never before

Days have gone by. I can tell I'm bouncing back
Darkness is no more and barrenness? ... is in lack.
I'm FILLED with joy, peace, and long-lasting smiles.
Now, THIS is the BEST I've felt in a while
Joy has become my declared decree
Regret has NO sting
Depression no longer owns me
Confusion has been replaced by confident esteem.
At last, my world is centered again,
Balanced by His mercy and His grace
... with prayer, devotionals, worship, and praise,
My hope has returned ... and so has my faith.
Here I am, living life with purpose, renewed
Hurts and pain of my past-in rear view

FOCUSED-with clarity, I've got a made-up mind!!

DETERMINED-to cling to hope and light-REFUSING to let go THIS time

I will fight with all I am-understanding that trials will come.

I will fight with all I am-recognizing He's caused me to overcome,

Counting UP the cost,

Calling it ALL a loss,

Exchanging WHAT I lost,

For the TRIUMPHANT reward of the cross,

    I... HAVE ... THE ... VICTORY!!

©2021 Tize Symplrix Williams

PART II

Week Twenty-Seven

The Miracle

My Testimony Part 2

¹⁴ Is any sick among you? Let him call for the elders of the church; and let them pray over him, anointing him with oil in the name of the Lord: ¹⁵ And the prayer of faith shall save the sick, and the Lord shall raise him up....

James 5:14-15

My son Christian spent the first four and a half months of his life in a hospital snuggled tightly in a well-knitted blanket that had been handmade by one of the Catholic sisters that would visit from time to time. He was housed in a warm incubator that seemed almost as tiny as he was. I am told that on one particular occasion, when my mother was called by the hospital to tell her that Christian had a setback and that he probably wouldn't make it through the night because, among other things, they had discovered a hole in his heart and thought he could have bleeding in his brain so they needed to get there as soon as possible so he wouldn't have to die alone. Since I was in another hospital still struggling with my health issues, they thought it best for them not to contact me but reach out to my mother instead. My mother recalls my aunt saying when she called to deliver the news, "Ain't no babies dying tonight, and I'm going back to bed!" Well, heaven must have heard that declaration loud and clear because though I can't be sure if any other babies died in the world that night, I can attest that mine didn't!

When Heaven Speaks

I have heard many people pay homage to the grandmothers and mothers who prayed for them throughout the years. Well, not only did I have a praying grandmother and mother, I had a praying aunt who was not afraid to bank a big fat one to the enemy's forehead. Aunt Gin was bold and audacious when it came to the things of God. The next day, as I am told, they both went into Children's Hospital on a mission – to lay healing hands on the then-sickly little one. Unbeknownst to the neonatal staff and nurses, aunt Gin had sneaked a small vile of anointed oil in his room and put a small dab of it on her index finger, then stuck her hand in his incubator and touched his head. She and my mother prayed the prayer of healing and wholeness over my son! To this day, I don't know for sure if it was the laying on of hands, God's sovereignty and mercy, or both (I'm thinking it was both) that healed my baby that day. What I do know with all certainty is that he was healed!

When he was well enough and had reached the 5lb mark, which was a major milestone for him, I was finally able to bring my baby home. It was an adjustment because they sent him home with not only a small oxygen tank but an apnea monitor as well. So, you can imagine sleep for me was pretty much non-existent. Between watching to make sure his heart didn't stop and whether or not he was gasping for air, my nights were long and restless, to say the least. The doctors had planned for long-term care for him. However, at his very first follow-up appointment, the doctors tested him to see how well he would do breathing on his own. To their amazement, he did it! My baby was breathing on his own with no help from the oxygen. And his heart rate was normal. They asked me to stay longer so they could monitor him some more. They were expecting something to go awry, and they would have to connect him back up to all the gadgets. But God had performed a miracle. In astonishment, the doctor called another doctor in. Before I knew it, nurses and more doctors came to see this miracle. They had not expected such a quick recovery on a premature child with such a bad prognosis. But, when God's healing hands touch a circumstance, and He breaths His breath of life into your situation, it leads to a downpour of promise, potential, and possibilities!

Today, at age 25, Christian is alive and well. Somehow, that hole that was in his heart miraculously closed on its own, so he never needed surgery to repair it, and he has never had an issue. He has never had a speech problem, never had respiratory problems, or any issues with his motor skills. He developed a love, almost an obsession even, for basketball at a young age and played little league for years. Then in junior high and senior high school, he played football. Never having any medical issues as a result. From the beginning, he was always a BIG miracle in a very small package.

Do you realize that miracles happen every day of our lives? There's probably one happening right now. They are the rare, impossible to mortal man, unexplainable happenings. They are providential occurrences that transcend the laws of physics and gravity because they are orchestrated by the Deity. Think back over your life, at where you've been; the tight spots, the low places, the dark pits, and recall how if God hadn't spared your life and protected you, life as you know it would be much different. How many times has God had to breathe His breath of life into you and your family? So many times, we forget to thank God for the small miracles that are right in front of us-the ones that happen every day. If you put all of your trust in him, no matter how dire the situation or how frightened you become, you will not regret it one bit. I urge you to put your faith in the sovereign King. He will be with you in every storm, walk with you through every valley, calm all your fears, and wipe away every tear.

My Inspiration: "Miracles start to happen when you give as much energy to your dreams as you do to your fears".
~ Richard Wilkins

HEAVEN SPEAKS TO ME: Who in your life do you think will benefit from hearing your testimony? How can you share your testimony with others to help them in their walk with Christ? How did these experiences increase your faith?

_____
_____
_____
_____
_____
_____
_____
_____
_____
_____
_____
_____
_____

Scripture Reading: Psalm 139:13-14; Matthew 17:20; 2 Kings 20:5; Acts 4:30

PRAYER: Father God, my life has not been perfect by far. The experiences I've had has not all been great, but I know that there is purpose in everything you allow us to go through. Help me not be ashamed or afraid to share my testimony with others so they, too, can know the power of your grace and their hope strengthened in you. Amen!

Week Twenty-Eight

Mirror, Mirror!

> [23] *Anyone who listens to the word but does not do what it says is like someone who looks at his face in a mirror* [24] *and, after looking at himself, goes away and immediately forgets what he looks like.* [25] *But whoever looks intently into the perfect law that gives freedom and continues in it—not forgetting what they have heard, but doing it—they will be blessed in what they do.*
>
> **James 1:22, 25 (NIV)**

Christian must have been about 10 or 11 when the incident happened. On any given day, my yard would be filled with several rambunctious boys enjoying each other's company and wreaking with the smells of wet puppies. My son was always the main attraction, and the neighborhood kids just loved playing with him. On the weekends he would spend with his father, his little buddies would come rushing to the door with excitement, only to leave with hung-down heads of sadness when I informed them that he wasn't there. "Well, when will he be back," they would demand to know! Then I would hear, "Awh, man! He's not coming back for two whole days." Then I would watch them mope around as if they had no hope of having a good day without him.

One day, one of his friends came banging on the door. I jumped up, and the little guy could hardly speak or breathe. He had run the whole way and was panting. I asked what it was, and he said, 'Christian is hurt!" I asked what happened. Without answering, he replied, "he's hurt really bad!" I could see the fright in his eyes, and suddenly, my heart began to pound. He said he was down the street, so I asked him to show me where. I didn't realize he meant way, way down the street and around the corner. When we reached the corner where Christian was, I began to pant, gasping for much-needed air. I stopped to catch my breath, but the little guy kept running. As I looked down the street, I saw a crowd of people hovering over someone. Fear gripped me, and from somewhere, I got my second wind, and I sprinted the rest of the way. When I got there, all I could see was blood. So, so much blood. I was horrified.

He had done what I repeatedly told him not to do. He tried jumping the curb with his bike. When the front wheel didn't clear the curb, it jammed right into it instead, sending Christian flying face-first to the concrete. His face had hit the ground so hard he was not even recognizable. The swelling was so massive. One of the neighbors was attending to him until I got there and agreed to take me back to the house. Without thinking to call and wait for the ambulance, my adrenalin was pumping so hard and fast, I wrapped his whole head in a towel, and away I zoomed to the nearest hospital, which fortunately was only about ten minutes away.

Upon leaving the hospital the next day, he left with a head wrap to keep the swelling down and to allow his face to heal properly. Thankfully, after many brain scans, there was no concussion or brain swelling, which the doctors were amazed to find due to the impact of the incident. For weeks, I made sure to redress the head wrap and administer an adequate dose of meds. I also tried to ensure he didn't peak and look at his face because I knew that wouldn't go well. And, wouldn't you know it, he did it anyway. I heard a loud distress call. I ran upstairs, and he was in the mirror, completely terrified at what he saw. He kept saying, "my face, mom, my face"! He was in total panic mode. He thought he would look like that forever and kids wouldn't want to be friends with him. He said, "I looked ugly, like a monster." Though he may have seen a monster's face, I just saw my son with a swollen face. I assured him that it wouldn't be like that always and that once the swelling went down, he would be back to normal.

Have you looked in the mirror lately? Were you terrified at the image the enemy portrayed? Did he pose a portrait of every dark place you've been in your life? Every bad decision you've made? How about that bad deed you did years ago that he just won't allow you to forget? Well, he's just doing his job. Satan's job is to paint the worst picture of your life, your failures, all of your mistakes, and every bad decision you have ever made. He steals, kills, and tries to destroy every good thing God has placed inside of you. He wants you to see a condemned soul staring back at you. A hopeless, good-for-nothing man and father. A worthless woman, not fit to be a mother or a wife. The leader who no one wants to follow. Or the child that no one wants to love. No matter what portrait Satan flashes in front of you, remember that he is a liar, and the truth is not in him!

When we go against what God's word says and try doing things on our own, we will make a mess out of it every time. Don't give the enemy any ammunition to use against you. He knows when we've been disobedient, and he will make sure we don't forget it; while continuing to convince us to do things our way, knowing full well it won't end well for us. That's because he's a deceiver of the saints! Let the word of God be your mirror. Instead of spending so much time in front of the mirror that Satan built, comparing yourself to the rest of the world and reminiscing on how you used to look and what you used to have, try flipping through some scripture. Examine yourself through the mirror of the Almighty, your creator and the One who makes all things, people, and circumstances well. Go ahead and take a look in the mirror. Is what you see fair? Is it whole? Is the image staring back at you well with your soul? If not, then you are looking in a counterfeit mirror.

My Inspiration: Do you want to meet the love of your life? Look in the mirror.
~ Byron Katie

HEAVEN SPEAKS TO ME: *Take some time to self-reflect. What image do you see when you look in the mirror? Do you see your past sins, hurts, and failures? Or do you see yourself in light of the word? Now that you have changed mirrors, what changes have you noticed?*

_____
_____
_____
_____
_____
_____
_____
_____
_____
_____
_____

Scripture Reading: 1 Corinthians 11:28, Ephesians 4:22-24, 2 Corinthians 3:18, Isaiah 43:18-19

PRAYER: Lord, you are a God of new beginnings. Thank you for helping me to only reflect on my past but continue to look forward to what you have in store for me. I thank you that you have made me whole; so that now when I look in the mirror, I see more of you and less of me and the sins of my past. You are truly faithful and just to forgive. Help me to always embrace your forgiveness and learn to forgive myself, also. Amen!

Week Twenty-Nine

Colors

◆◆◆◆◆◆◆◆◆◆

And God said, Let us make man in our image, after our likeness: and let them have dominion...

Genesis 1:26

The year was 1988 when the movie Colors hit the big screen starring Robert Duvall and Sean Penn. Having grown up in South Central Los Angeles, I can remember this time vividly as gang violence and drive-by shootings were on the rise in that area and around the country. The movie depicted a hot-headed rookie and a veteran trying to show him the ropes in the gang-ridden streets of LA. The character of Danny (played by Sean Penn) quickly earned himself a reputation with the gangs, and before it was all said and done, he had to come to grips with his own racism. Ironically, he falls in love with a Hispanic girl.

Red and blue were often forbidden depending on what set you claimed and who you claimed had much to do with what block you lived on. Colors mattered whether you agreed with it or not. The gangs that controlled many of those LA streets thought it mattered to the point that they were often willing to inflict pain on those who opposed it. In all actuality, your choice of colors just might be the deciding factor on whether you were harassed, beaten, killed, or maybe all of the above.

When I was in about the 5th grade, I was bussed out to a "valley school." Things were getting pretty rough in the LA schools, so my mother thought it best to send me to Parthenia Elementary school in Northridge, CA. I recall some of my friends from the block ragging me about it.

After several months of being at the new school, I was told that I thought I was special and asked why I was trying to talk "white." I still don't really know what talking white means. I guess if you use proper English, that's talking white. Maybe? It was even said that I liked white people better than I did my "own" kind. How ludicrous! It has nothing to do with color, and even today, all those many years later, we are still making a big deal over color and race.

The bible tells us that we are all created in the image of God, male and female (vs. 27), and when God saw everything that he made, behold, it was very good (vs. 31). We are all created in God's good image- black, white, yellow, and red. When God created man, He deemed it as good.

Notice how it didn't say only whites or blacks are created in my image. He did not specify what race of man. He simply said, "Let us make man." When God created Adam and Eve, their ethnicity was never once mentioned. This omission signifies that the word man was all-inclusive for every man regardless of race. They are considered the mother and father of all people of all ethnicities. Therefore, they are non-ethnic with no specific nationality. Why? Because they represent all people of every race, ethnicity, and nationality. We all have equal status and are all equally unique in our way. That's the beauty of humanity. All of our existence add value to the human race.

God's love and compassion have no color because He is no respecter for the persons (Acts 10:34-35). The love of Christ must be carried across all ethnic lines. In Christ, we are all unified together. There is no differentiating between races and nationalities. As believers, our identity ought not to be based on our skin color but on our adoption into the family of God.

This new identity in Christ overshadows all other identities. We stand unified as one body under a great God who loves and cares for us all. It is the love of God and the truth of the gospel of Jesus Christ that draws us closer to each other and Him by filling in the gaps and breaking all barrier-divides.

In the parable of the Good Samaritan (Luke 10:25-37), the whole premise is the idea that loving your neighbor as yourself is inclusive of loving those neighbors who are different and don't look anything like us.

The bible does not speak on merely tolerating other ethnic groups but rather truly loving them. This entails a total coming together, complete unity among the body of Christ. If the truth is told, we haven't dealt with this issue of race because we clearly don't understand the power of God's grace.

When we see Jesus face to face, I can assure you He won't be putting the blacks to the right, whites to the left, Asians and Hispanics in the middle, and so forth. We will be standing side by side, arms locked together in love, singing, worshipping, and praising our King. When all God's children come together as one, that is when God will be glorified on the earth, and all of heaven will rejoice!

My Inspiration: Prejudice is a burden that confuses the past, threatens the future, and renders the present inaccessible.
~ Maya Angelou.

HEAVEN SPEAKS TO ME: Racial tensions are on the rise. How have you been affected by it due to the color of your skin? Have you treated others differently because of their skin color? What has God spoken to your heart about race relations through His Word?

_____
_____
_____
_____
_____
_____
_____
_____
_____
_____

Scripture Reading: Revelations 7:9, 14:6, Colossians 3:11, Ephesians 2:14-16; Leviticus 19:34

PRAYER: Just and merciful God, ALL of your precious creations were created in your beautiful image. Help us to see the beauty of you in others no matter how difficult they make it. Teach us to love You first, then ourselves, so that we can also love each other as you have commanded us regardless of color, gender, nationality, or religious and political beliefs. Amen!

Week Thirty

The IT Factor

Prayer, Praise, Worship, the WORD

*Glory in his holy name; let the heart of them rejoice that seek the LORD."
Seek the LORD and his strength; seek his face continually!*

1 Chronicles 16:10-11

As a young, flippant college student, I was very opinionated and thought I had an answer for everything. I was always on the defense and tended to have a combative air about myself. I wanted people to know that they couldn't just say anything they wanted to me and get away with it. One day as I was waiting for a friend after class. As I sat there, a young man came and sat next to me, and we struck up a conversation. He didn't know what he was getting himself into.

We began talking about relationships and how guys approach women, and how women often respond. After a lot of ado about nothing at all, he said something that rubbed me the wrong way. He told me that I didn't have the "It Factor," and that was why I didn't have anyone special in my life. Of course, this was after I brushed him off after his own poorly executed advances. He went on to tell me that relationships all boiled down to people knowing what works for them and what doesn't. Now, when I think of that, it's kind of true in many areas of life.

When we experience turbulent times, so often, we make turning to Jesus the last resort. We tend to try everything else first in a sad attempt to try and fix things on our own. We try calling other people; parents, a loyal confidant, our best friend, the mailman, the milkman, the bum on the corner. Anyone who will listen to our sad stories.

But what if we discovered our spiritual "it factor?" What if we made it a habit of turning, no running, to Jesus whenever things started going sideways in our lives? What if we made prayer, praise, worship, and the word our "it?" Imagine how much better we would feel, how much more at peace we would be. Let's take worship, for instance. When you pray, you talk to God about what you know about, right? But when you worship God, he can fix the things you don't know about, so the best place to run to is His presence, where he knows about everything before we even tell him about it. He knows that thing that would have, should have, could have happened to you, but it didn't. Why? Because He was protecting and shielding you from dangers seen and unseen, like only He can.

I remember hearing someone who was very much stuck in religion say that they only wanted to hear the word preached because they thought praise and worship were just all about entertainment. Shame on them! To say that you only get to church in time for the word is to say you don't understand that the word is for us. But worship, now that's for Him. To intentionally miss the worship service because you don't like the group whose singing or because you don't like the song lineup is not only foolish and immature, but it also says that you don't care about what God wants and you're not interested in giving him his due worship.

When our backs get against a wall, or we are stuck between a rock and a hard place, what foundation will you stand on? Will you get caught in your feelings and only what you want? Or, will you shift your thinking and break free from the mindset that it's all about me and turn to what we all know works-prayer, praise, worship, and the unadulterated word of God? We need it all!

When we do these things, chains are broken, and strongholds are loosed. The enemy can't stand when we pray to tear down his demonic kingdom. Satan hates when we worship our God. Our praise and worship ushers in the presence of God. His presence can't enter where there is no praise and or worship. We should be able to declare what Job said, "Though you slay me yet will I trust you" (Job 13:15).

Sadly, this is usually not our default thinking process as humans. But, as believers, it ought to be our sure stance. Life is not always good, but our God sure is. When the mountain doesn't move, pray for strength to push it out of your way. If the giant doesn't stand down, speak the Word with power to defeat and slay it. And, when your breakthrough just won't come, worship. If you want His presence in your life and your circumstances to change, then I encourage you to find your "it factor" and work it until your change comes.

My Inspiration: Any man or woman on this earth who is bored and turned off by worship is not ready for heaven.
~ A.W. Tozer

HEAVEN SPEAKS TO ME: What or who do you run to when trouble comes your way? What spiritual factors do you consider when chaos comes? Which "it factor" that was discussed do you find works best for you (the word, prayer, praise, or worship)?

_____

_____

_____

_____

_____

_____

_____

_____

_____

_____

_____

_____

Scripture Reading: Job 13:15; Psalms 150:1-6, Psalms 100:2; Hebrews 13:15

PRAYER: Dear God, thank you so much for the desire to pray, praise, worship, and read your holy word. I understand that it is when I practice these things consistently that things change for my good, and I experience your continued presence in my life. Help me to always cling to you and your word in the good days and the bad. May I always read your word daily, keep praise on my lips, have true worship in my heart, and pray without ceasing. Amen.

Week Thirty-One

When God Chooses You

Also, I heard the voice of the Lord, saying: "Whom shall I send, And who will go for Us?" Then I said, "Here am I! Send me." ⁹And He said, "Go, and tell this people....

Isaiah 6:8-9

Can you imagine being the one chosen out of hundreds, thousands, or even millions of other people to do God's bidding? The feeling of importance you would feel. You'd think how special you were to have been chosen over and above everyone else. I know I sure did. I was chosen to travel to Barcelona, Spain, with a company that I was doing some contract work for some years back. They brought me on to help with the marketing for their global sales conference.

The company, an international organization with offices all over the world on several continents, was not getting the results from another company they had hired to do all the "heavy lifting" in terms of organizing this event. Well, they had missed several deadlines, and for all the thousands of dollars they were being paid, my boss at the time it was tired of dealing with that company and felt we were not getting our monies worth. So, he suggested that I, a contract worker, go instead to ensure everything ran smoothly since I was doing so much anyway. The company had to pay $300 to expedite my passport as we were leaving in just two weeks.

The mere thought of me going to Barcelona, Spain, at no cost was unfathomable. But, I had been chosen, not some of the other people who were actual company employees, but little old me—a contract worker. If truth be told, I may have even started to think I was somebody because of it. I probably even had a little pride or perhaps even some arrogance to build upon the inside because I was chosen!

Have you ever experienced that? You were ready and waiting, and as a result, they saw your readiness and observed how prepared you were; then, it came down the pipeline that you were the one, the chosen one. Did you know that as a born-again believer, you have also been chosen by the creator, the God of the universe? Your name has been called, and you heard through the grapevine that God was looking for someone to, Go to, and you heeded the call.

Webster defines chosen as one who is the object of choice or one of divine favor: an elect person. Being chosen is not just about being favored, but it comes with a requirement to act responsibly. God's favor comes with some conditions, as recorded in Exodus 19:5, "Now if you obey me fully and keep my covenant, then out of all nations you will be my treasured possession." The bible further attests to these requirements when he says, "Since God chose you to be the holy people he loves, you must clothe yourselves with tenderhearted mercy, kindness, humility, gentleness, and patience" (Col. 3:12, NLT).

When God is looking for someone to choose to do His bidding, he is not looking for perfection or someone with high social status; he is looking for a willing vessel. Someone yielded with a posture of total surrender to his will and purpose. Often when God is looking for someone to go, we are too busy ducking and dodging him, as if he doesn't already see us right in our hiding places, that we miss out on the move he is trying to make in and around our lives. We completely miss him because of our unwillingness to yield. When we are ready and waiting for him to bellow out the call for service, we can say what Isaiah said, "I heard the voice of the

Lord, saying, "Whom shall I send? And who will go for us?" And I said, "Here am I. Send Me!"

Thankfully, it doesn't stop there. Some benefits come along with being chosen. When I was chosen to travel for business across the great seas, it gave me a new experience. A chance to visit a place I had never even dreamed of going to. It allowed me to make new friends from far away places that I still have to this day. But the benefits God gives to his chosen are far greater. As God's chosen, we get constant reminders of his great love for us. It means we have a standing invitation to dine with him in our secret place. We have a sense of divine purpose that we didn't have before. It allows us to make a brand new connection with sovereignty. And it provides a new perspective and gives the concept of freedom a whole new meaning.

Live each day knowing that you are chosen by God to do great things. Do not take it lightly but be intentional about each task given to you, knowing that with being God's elect comes the responsibility of clothing ourselves every day with what brings him joy—us choosing to be kind, showing mercy, being gentle, and walking in humility before him.

My Inspiration: When God has selected you, it doesn't matter who else has rejected or neglected you. God's favor outweighs all opposition. You are a winner!
~ **Unknown**

HEAVEN SPEAKS TO ME: Think back on a time when you were not chosen. Explain how it made you feel. What was your initial reaction? How does knowing what God says about you change your response to being overlooked?

_____
_____
_____
_____
_____
_____
_____
_____
_____
_____
_____
_____
_____

Scripture Reading: Psalm 4:3; Deuteronomy 7:6; Colossians 3:12-17; Matthew 22:14

PRAYER: Lord God, thank you for each opportunity to serve You. Thank You for putting me in the right places at the right time. Help me to always be a yielded vessel ready to go whenever and wherever you want me to and without complaint. Prepare my mind, body, and spirit to walk confidently into every territory that you lead me into, knowing full well that you are always with me. Amen!

Week Thirty-Two

The Despair of Delay

◆◆◆◆◆◆◆◆◆

*Hope deferred makes the heart sick, But
a longing fulfilled is a tree of life*

Proverbs 13:12

We spend a lot of time waiting in our lives for one thing or another. I know I have personally spent most of my life waiting for something. I've waited for an answer. I've waited for a sign. I've waited for directions. I've waited for healing, and the list could go on and on of the things I have and am still waiting for. I don't have the answer to why God often makes us wait. I do, however, believe that there is purpose and power in waiting.

The wait builds character and often teaches us lessons we wouldn't otherwise have learned. It also makes us stronger. But more than anything, I believe the wait makes us worship. When we worship while we wait, it compels us to see God for who he is despite the outcome not being what we hoped for or whether our prayers are answered in the way we thought they would be. Even still, knowing that worshipping is the absolute best response to waiting doesn't make it any less daunting. What I have come to realize, though, is that worship properly redirects our focus on God's ability to make a way when there is none. It helps us to set our sights on things above and the absolute power that he has instead of focusing on the uncertain road ahead of us. Worship reassures us that we can trust that God is working on our behalf while we wait.

In addition to worshipping, we should also trust God in the wait. Serve others while we patiently wait. Be watchful and expectant while waiting. And we must have an attitude of gratitude while we wait for God to show up in our situation. With thanksgiving, we must take the time to thank the giver of all things. Listen, our lives will not change until we do.

Let's look at Psalms 42. This psalm, or should I say a sincere prayer, is from a very discontented saint, which I can relate to. If you're honest, you can too. Though the reference was made, David did not long for water like the deer, but rather, the psalmist used the analogy of the deer panting for the water brook to paint a very powerful picture of his dire need to be in communion with God. Like a thirsty deer panting for water, his very soul was thirsting for more of God. To be in his presence. He viewed communion as a great necessity and not just a mere luxury. When we reach that level of hunger, any turmoil and turbulence we may encounter will only be seen as minor setbacks instead of major catastrophes.

David, while in the midst of his lamenting, cried out to God, saying, "My tears have been my meat day and night, while they continually say unto me, where is your God (vs 3)? But I love how even in sorrow, David was still able to worship his God. He had been waiting for deliverance for what seemed like an eternity but was still able to trust in God's ability to deliver and set him free. David encouraged himself in the Lord by saying, "Yet the Lord will command his lovingkindness in the daytime, and in the night his song shall be with me, and my prayer unto the God of my life (vs. 8). Then he goes on to tell himself, "Hope thou in God; for I shall yet praise him, who is the help of my countenance, and my God."

There are many benefits to waiting on God. We are protected from dangers unseen when we wait. We learn more about God's character when we wait. And it allows God to show us who we are and what we are capable of. Waiting on God helps us to focus on the purpose and direction of our lives according to God's will. It's important to take time to be still before God, falling deeply into Him, so we confidently know God's will as we live out our daily lives, being dependent on him to see us through whichever dry place we may find ourselves in.

Simply put, waiting on God is not a time to despair, but it should draw us closer to him. When we draw nigh to him, he will draw nigh to us to carry us through.

My Inspiration: As I look back on my life, I realize that every time I thought I was being REJECTED from something good, I was actually being RE-DIRECTED to something better
~ **Steve Maraboli**

HEAVEN SPEAKS TO ME: Name something you have been waiting for. What has been your attitude while you have waited? How has reading this devotional changed your perspective on waiting? How will you wait going forward?

_____
_____
_____
_____
_____
_____
_____
_____
_____
_____
_____
_____
_____

Scripture Reading: Psalms 130:5; 1 Corinthians 1:7; Psalms 37:7; 2 Peter 3:9; Luke 18:7

PRAYER: Gracious God, no matter what I may face ahead, I want to place my trust in You alone. Give me the strength to faithfully and patiently wait on You to move to the next phase in my life. I know without a doubt that your plans are good. When I become impatient, give me renewed strength to continue. When I become tired, please comfort me as only You can. Help me, Father God, to trust You wholeheartedly at all times and remind me that faith in you is never wasted. Amen!

Week Thirty-Three

Faith Shakers

Now faith is confidence in what we hope for and assurance about what we do not see.

NIV Hebrews 11:1

Having lived my formative years in the state of California, I grew very familiar with earthquakes and the effects they could have on an otherwise stable foundation. There were a couple of instances when I was in class, and a sudden shaking would occur. Then the mandate to get under our desks would soon follow until the shaking ceased, and it was clear to emerge from our temporary safe havens. I can't even imagine the fear of being in the midst of a major earthquake. Over the years, there have been several notable earthquakes that claimed thousands of lives. I can remember the quakes in both Mexico (2017) and Haiti (2010) and the devastation they both caused. I think it's safe to say that earthquakes are serious business and can shake not only the earth but human beings to our very core. Sometimes, even the aftershocks can be damaging.

Similarly, our faith, too, can be shaken to its core, and our foundation can become rattled and unstable. Our lives are no different. Life consists of all kinds of twists and turns, ups and downs, and ins and outs. No matter how efficient we are at planning out our lives at every stage and age, life still tends to throw us curve balls that we can never be prepared for. With no warning, our quiet lives are interrupted with trembling and unwanted abrupt movements and tremors that we never bargained for. These sudden shifts in our foundation can come in a series of waves that occur because of volcanic undercurrents and disturbances that erupts without our permission. The result can be total devastation.

Even David, being a man after God's own heart (Acts 13:22), yet, became discouraged. Struggles, disappointments, and depression doesn't care what side of town you live on or how padded and deep your pockets are, or even how spiritual you are. I believe God allows faith-shakers to occur in our lives to ultimately develop unshakable faith in us. When our faith is unshakable, our desire for God increases. When our desire for him increases, we seek more of him, and we obtain more of him (Jeremiah 29:13). He then reigns in us. In time, the kingdom of God will become a part of who we are. If the kingdom of God is in us, and that kingdom is unshakable and unmovable, then guess what? We to become unshakable and unmovable and always abounding in his good works (1 Cor. 15:58). Being unshakable and unmovable is to be steadfast with a sure stance of your belief that God is greater than any adversity that may come our way.

Even in those times when we can't see our way or a way out of whatever we are in, we must trust. As we take our minds off of our issues and set our eyes on God, we no longer allow ourselves to be affected by the chaos around us. When we lean into God and the comfort that his word brings into our very existence and situation, we become strengthened, confident, and empowered to do all things through Christ, who is giving us strength (Philippians 4:13). As we read the word of God, bask in His presence, and learn to pray the promises, our faith becomes so strong, unaltered, and unshakable that not even a tsunami of a trial will be able to sway us from trusting and total dependency on God. Because God's promises are unbreakable, our hope and faith can also be.

My Inspiration: Faith is not believing in my own unshakeable belief. Faith is believing an unshakable God when everything in me trembles and quakes
~ **Beth Moore**

HEAVEN SPEAKS TO ME: Describe a time when your faith was shaken. Since that time, how has your faith grown? Name two defining moments when you knew your faith had become unshakable. In what way(s) have you learned to develop unshakable faith?

_____
_____
_____
_____
_____
_____
_____
_____
_____
_____

Scripture Reading: Hebrews 11 (read in its entirety); James 2:14-26; Ephesians 3:16-17; Romans 1:17

PRAYER: Faithful God, you are a God of grace and great strength. Yet, I get weak and very sorrowful when life gets hard. Sometimes I forget your word and can't think straight because I am overwhelmed and unstable in my faith. But I know it is in these times when your strength is made perfect in my weakness. Help me, Lord, to take the faith stand no matter how I feel or what I see. Help me to allow myself to fall ever so willingly into your mighty arms of grace. Help me to develop unshakable faith and hope in You. Amen!

Week Thirty-Four

Stimulus Package

◆◆◆◆◆◆◆◆◆

Save now, I pray, O LORD;
O LORD, I pray, send now prosperity!

Psalms 118:25, NKJV

The year 2020 will go down in the history books as a tumultuous year to remember. Photographed in the hearts and minds of every human being who is of age will be the 12 months and beyond of a deadly virus that paralyzed the world. Fear, uncertainty, anxiety, depression, sadness, and fright are all emotions that were felt by one person or another during that time. Some are still reeling from the effects of COVID-19. Whether we had to deal with being infected by the virus or have lost someone near and dear to us because of it, we have all been touched in some way.

In addition to the physical and psychological effects was the financial mayhem that it caused. Jobs were lost, homes foreclosed, and families were thrown out of their safe havens, often without adequate warning. It was one of the deadliest and scariest times, and we, the people, needed help and fast. We needed emotional relief and a financial reprieve from all of the losses we had experienced. We needed to be stimulated! Our pockets and bank accounts alike needed it. Our health and our homes needed it! Most of all, we needed our very hearts and souls stimulated! Even though that may have been the last thing on many people's minds, or maybe it had become the first since there was such a great need, we all needed something.

The government's response to some of the issues was money. They issued several payouts to all qualifying Americans. This payout was to help get the economy stimulated and moving forward again. These highly anticipated payouts were coined "stimulus checks." Some would say these payouts are what helped to keep them afloat. There were even humorous Gifs, songs, and videos asking the question, "Are you stimulating yet" in other words, have you received your check yet. I love how we can sometimes find humor even in more dire situations. But, while we may have needed a boost financially, what God was saying to us is that we needed to be shaken and stimulated by more of Him, not a check from the government. We were in crisis, and the only One we needed to look to was and still is Jesus!

In the book of Psalms, David urges the Lord to send help in times of need. He prayed how we all ought to pray, with a true sense of urgency. He prayed, *"Save now, I pray Oh Lord, Oh Lord I pray send prosperity now!"* We often think of prosperity in terms of money. But I can assure you that in the middle of a pandemic, people are more concerned about their health and the safety of their loved ones. Though money can purchase many things, it can't buy us life and certainly not eternal life. That is only found by confessing to our Lord and Savior, Jesus Christ. Romans 10:10 tells us that if we *"Confess with our mouth, Jesus is Lord, and believe in our hearts that God raised him from the dead, we shall be saved."*

It doesn't matter if you're a Ph.D., P.E., MD, Ed.D., or just a GED; we spend a lot of time and money to give ourselves and our lives a boost by oftentimes pursuing material things, things that are in actuality non-stimulants disguised as relevant essential needs. Our authentic successes are directly tied to who we know God to be in our lives and in times of lack and genuine need. If we permit ourselves to crave stimulation by things outside of God's will for our lives, we run the risk of God's anger being kindled against us (Numbers 11:31-34). When our spirits require a supernatural stimulus, we can set our eyes on the hilltops of heaven because it is from that place that our help will flow. We need to keep looking upward and not outward. When we look outward for what our souls are truly in need of, the supply soon runs out, and we are right back where we started. God's supply is never-ending. For as long as we keep looking to him to stimulate our inner man, so shall he continue to supply our every need.

My Inspiration: God's work done in God's way will never lack God's provision.
~ J. Hudson Taylor

HEAVEN SPEAKS TO ME: Think about what you crave. Do your taste buds align with God's word and will for your life? Write about a time when you knew your desires were contrary to God's plan for your life. In what ways are you learning to discipline yourself to ensure you only remain stimulated by God's truth and not the allures of the world?

_____

_____

_____

_____

_____

_____

_____

_____

_____

_____

Scripture Reading: Numbers 11:1-35; Proverbs 10:22; Philippians 4:19; Matthew 6:19-21; Hebrews 13:5

PRAYER: Jehovah Jireh, I thank you for who you are as my faithful Father, Lord, and my Provider. Your word is true, and you cannot lie. You promised to never leave nor forsake me and that you would supply all my needs according to your riches in glory. Thank you for being a promise keeper. I acknowledge your faithfulness in my life to meet all of my and my family's needs. I will never forget how you have always provided for me in the past, so I know, without a doubt, you will do it again and again. Amen!

Week Thirty-Five

Abundant Living Mandates Different Living

◆◆◆◆◆◆◆◆◆

The thief does not come except to steal, and to kill, and to destroy. I come that they might have life, and that they might have it more abundantly.

John 10:10

As a kid, I dreamed of having an abundance of success. I would fantasize about all the material things and money I would have and how I would help all the people in need. You see, I was a very generous kid. I didn't like seeing people hurting and going without. I still don't. It bothers me when I see a need and can't fill the need. My mind often goes back to how things were supposed to turn out, how I was supposed to live a life of abundance and be in a position to give to everyone. Though that was probably a lot of our dream as children, how many of us are living that abundant life today? If not, why aren't we? Did we stop having compassion for those in need? Did we allow selfishness and stinginess to seep into our hearts? Do we now have the spirit of hoarders that want to keep everything God blesses us with for ourselves? Lord forbid that we would become so self-absorbed that the needs of others are no longer an issue or priority in the life that God has so graciously allowed us to live.

What does it mean to live abundantly? Abundant life has to do with living life in abounding grace, joy, and strength through Jesus Christ and basking in the overflow of God's fullness. It's having more than enough of everything you need. A life of abundance is not just having stuff. When we live a life of abundance through Christ, we are intricately connected to the Source of everything that we will ever need and desire.

If we want to live an abundant lifestyle, we must alter our mode of operation. I believe it's our mindsets that need to shift. We must have a mind of gratitude for what God has already given us. It should be a mindset of one living in the fullness of God's grace and abundant blessings and being good stewards of those blessings. Have you ever observed a wealthy person? They tend to carry themselves differently than the average Joe Blow from the street. A woman who totes a $20,000 Prada bag wouldn't be seen just throwing, or sitting it for that matter, on the ground, unlike someone who purchased their purse from the local Walmart. Nor would someone who lives in a $5 million mansion wouldn't allow someone to write graffiti all over the outside of the house and throw beer cans and candy paper on the lawn, would they? It's a different mindset that makes them walk, talk, and act differently. Likewise, when we shouldn't just take what God has given to us and squander it, using it for frivolous thrills that neither help to build God's kingdom nor leaves a legacy for our family. When you have God's abundant grace and you are living in His fullness, your demeanor should be different from that of the world. You ought to maintain a perpetual attitude of gratitude. This God-given abundance is grace that comes from and through Christ Jesus. 2 Corinthians 8:9 tells us, "You know the grace of our Lord Jesus Christ, that though he was rich, yet for your sake, he became poor so that you through his poverty might become rich."

Take some downtime and visualize your success story. Allow yourself to see the abundant future God has predestined for you. The time has passed for making excuses for not maximizing the potential God has given each of us and cultivating the gifts He has so graciously placed in our hands. He has generously given us all talents as well as the power to obtain wealth (Deuteronomy 8:18).

If we can ever learn to create an atmosphere of abundant living instead of poverty and lack, understand that obtaining and maintaining abundance is a lifelong process that positions you for more. When God allows us to live abundantly and in the overflow, then it is our responsibility to leave a legacy of generosity for our loved ones. Stinginess is a great deterrent to abundant living. God is not pleased when we hoard his blessings and refuse to share what He has given us. Why hold on to material things and money that can easily be here today and gone tomorrow? One big house fire or one devastating crash of the stock market and all your earthly possession can be gone in the blink of an eye. The blessings of God don't bring sorrow. His blessings make us rich in every area of our lives; our health, finances, relationships, and much more (*Proverbs 10:22*). Abundant living is God's plan for His people.

Permit yourself to have a mindset shift. Change your mode of operating and live like you are blessed and living in the overflow of God's grace and abundance. Start giving and sharing more. Begin to show more kindness to random people. Let them see the love of Jesus in your life and generosity. Spread the joy of abundance with someone else today.

My Inspiration: Fear for the future makes people settle for things in the present that completely defy abundant life.

~ Beth Moore

HEAVEN SPEAKS TO ME: Share how living in God's fullness of grace has changed your life? What impact has living the abundant life He has given you impacted your and your family's life? In what why's can you share the abundance you have obtained through a relationship with Christ with others?

_____
_____
_____
_____
_____
_____
_____
_____
_____
_____
_____

Scripture Reading: Ezekiel 36:24-38; Psalms 67:5-6; Malachi 3:10-12; Deuteronomy 28:12

PRAYER: Most gracious and eternal God, I thank you for your generosity towards me and my loved ones. Show me how I can be generous and share the abundance that you have given to me. Help me to gladly give to others and live daily in the overflow. May the fullness and abundance of your grace help me to change my way of thinking and living in a way that honors you always. Amen!

Week Thirty-Six

Show Biz

"Beware of the scribes, who like to walk around in long robes and like greetings in the marketplace [39] and have the best seats in the synagogues and the places of honor at feasts,....[40] and for a pretense make long prayers. They will receive the greater condemnation."

Mark 12:38-40

The limelight was simply not something that I ever craved. I've pretty much been a behind-the-scenes kind of person and have tried to avoid it altogether. In grade school, I remember being in a play I was chosen to have a significant role in. It was a Christmas play if my memory serves me correctly. I walked up to the center stage, brave and confident to deliver my well-practiced performance, and I froze. It was as if I were frozen stiff in time. Nothing came out, and I was paralyzed. The bright lights and all the eager parent-filled auditorium seats and cameras flashing suddenly terrified me to complete silence. Talking about stage fright! Where did all my confidence go? My bravery? My courage? The words and animated gestures I planned to do to help intensify my performance did a disappearing act on me. They did an Elvis move and left the building.

As frightening and embarrassing as that experience was for me, I still reflect on it. Why did that happen? In many ways, I sometimes wish I could have a do-over so I can show the world what I am made of and show off my talent and giftedness. I think of what it would be like to get all the accolades and pats on the back and have people tell me what a great performance I gave and ask when there would be an encore.

I may never get that particular opportunity again. I am nobody's actor by far. Other than wanting to be a news anchor, it was never my desire to be in front of anyone's camera. So why have I often wished for another chance to shine in front of an audience? Like so many of us, we want attention. While the desire for accolades and the opportunity to gloat is, well, irresistible to some; (as if it convinces the people around us of our worthiness to be), it is an awful display of humility. So, what exactly are we craving to be that we strive to keep ourselves in the limelight, putting all our focus on ourselves? Why is it that we often act as if we are the stars in every act of our lives when in actuality, God is the preeminent screenwriter, director, and producer of every scene? He is the One who deserves the limelight every day and all the time. Every play in the script of our lives would be a bust without Him coaching, encouraging, and leading us. When we ignore His cues, we miss out on the role of a lifetime and become "has-beens" when He wants to make us leading ladies. Beware of developing a performance-based Christianity. One that makes you feel the only way to thrive and obtain the praise of "people" is to be the center of attention. Luke tells us that if we exalt ourselves, putting ourselves on a pedestal, we will be humbled or brought low, but if we humble ourselves instead, God will exalt us (emphasis mine, vs. 14:11, ESV).

Any and everything that we do for God should be done in a spirit of humility before Him, not looking for anything in return except the assurance that your Heavenly Father will reward you justly in His timing for the authenticity of your "good" works. If we are doing things with the wrong motives and for selfish gain, then it's not good to work as unto God. Rather, it's done for vainglory, and no one should get the glory but Jesus Christ. Anyone else getting the glory is an idol, and the bible speaks explicitly about how he feels about and deals with people, even if it's you who set up idols in place of Him. Remember, He is a jealous God

(Exodus 20:2 -6). So, whatever you do, do it in spirit and truth, giving all glory and honor to God. Take yourself out of the limelight and put it back where it belongs, on our Savior!

My Inspiration: A great man is always willing to be little.
~ Ralph Waldo Emerson

HEAVEN SPEAKS TO ME: Think about how God is teaching you to live a life of humility. Name a time when you might have been a little puffed up in your ways. What lesson has God taught you about being humble rather than proud? How does walking in humility please God?

_____
_____
_____
_____
_____
_____
_____
_____
_____
_____

Scripture Reading: Luke 14:11; Matthew 5:15-16; Proverbs 13:11; Matthew 6:1

PRAYER: Gracious Father, thank you for continuing to teach me how to walk in humility. In those times when I struggle to take the high road because my flesh wants to lash out, your Holy Spirit is always there to whisper in my ear, causing me to respond in a God-pleasing way. Lord, help me to take the focus off of me and shine the light on You as the Lord over everything. Help me to follow your divine script and not the one the world has written for me to perform but to follow wholeheartedly the word you have written for me. Amen!

Week Thirty-Seven

Treasure Seekers

For where your treasure is, there will your heart be also.

Matthew 6:21

During a time long ago, when humans cooked their food instead of relying on a man in a box named Jack to prepare it for them, people grew, prepared, and preserved their food in earthen vessels that were used for storing, cooking, and serving food as well as for transporting a variety of liquids. In the bible days, pottery was a very vital and important part of people's everyday lives. This pottery was representative of plenty and the abundance of things they deemed precious and or valuable.

    Some years back, I was given a gift in a very nice decorative box. If you look at it, the box itself wasn't all that fancy, but it had artwork on it that made it stand out, so I decided to keep it. In that box, somewhere in my house, are some semi-important items; coins, the occasional dollar bill, spare keys, keys to locks that I can't even remember where or what they lock or unlock, but I'm too afraid to throw them out, for fear that once I do I will remember what lock they belonged to. Anyway, my point is we probably all have boxes with things in them that we cherish and hold near and dear to us. For some, it's a family heirloom or a special trinket given by a special friend. The importance of those things, however, dictates where we keep them; out in the open for all to see or hidden to ensure what's in them stays safe and secure from theft or the curious little hands that, well, just can't seem to help themselves because their curiosity got the best of them.

No matter what the item is, if it finds its way into the "special" category, we find ways to preserve its value and protect it from the elements to prevent damage. We may even invest money into its safekeeping by purchasing a safety deposit box, a safe, or a file cabinet to which no one else knows the code. If we are willing to go to those lengths to keep material and perishable things safe, how much more should we work to keep God's truth safe from being contaminated by carnal things and people?

I love reading Psalms 119-even though it's a very long chapter. It's filled with so many great nuggets. Verses ten and eleven read, "With my whole heart have I sought thee: O let me not wander from thy commandments." Thy word have I hid in mine heart, that I might not sin against thee". Then verse 162, "I rejoice at thy word, as one that finds great treasure" (NKJV). Here we have an example of how we are to cherish God's word and allow it to be engrafted in the innermost parts of our hearts and how we are to rejoice over it as if we have found great riches.

Can you imagine how you would feel if you stumbled on a big garbage bag of diamonds that someone else may have thought to be trash and discarded them? I don't think there would be a still joint in your body, and your joy would be heard 10 miles away; it would be so loud. You'd most likely run and tell all your family. Well, on second thought, maybe not the whole family. I think everyone has that one relative that's just a little bit suspect, so we won't tell them. Anyway, reading the word of God and receiving insight and revelation knowledge from God should make us so excited that we run and tell not only our family but friends, neighbors, coworkers, and yes, even the boss because they need a word; just let everyone else.

The next time you open your bible, read it with the expectation of receiving everything God desires to give you through His Holy Word. Ask him to allow you to read it with clarity and understanding. Ask for revelation knowledge that only he can give. Get excited because the next time you read God's word, you are about to be let in on some heavenly secrets that only those close to his word will be privy to. When you do, make sure you treat it like the great treasure it is. Believe me, it will change your life.

My Inspiration: God's word is not just to be heard and repeated; it is to be breathed, lived, and emulated with each action.
~ Steve Maraboli

HEAVEN SPEAKS TO ME: Have you ever found a piece of jewelry or some money that someone had dropped by mistake? Or, have you ever won a lot of money in a lottery or perhaps in a raffle? Describe how it made you feel? How did you react? How do you respond to reading the word of God?

_____

_____

_____

_____

_____

_____

_____

_____

_____

_____

_____

_____

_____

Scripture Reading: Psalm 119:162; 2 Corinthians 4:7; Philippians 4:4; Habakkuk 3:17-18

PRAYER: Most gracious King! Giver of life, thank you for your living word. It is through your word that I find the strength and courage to keep moving forward. It's by your spoken word that my faith has been increased, and by your Holy word, I find my purpose. Help me to always rejoice in your Word. Amen!

<u>Week Thirty-Eight</u>

The Power of a Word

◆◆◆◆◆◆◆◆◆◆

Death and life are in the power of the tongue: and they that love it shall eat the fruit thereof.

Proverbs 18:21

"Sticks and stones may break my bones, but words never hurt me." Most of us are familiar with that cliché, right? But it's furthest from the truth. Words do hurt and can be downright devastating. I can't count the times that I have had someone speak words to me that hurt deeply, words that belittled and were dogmatic in every way. Yet there were moments when I wasn't allowed to say a word back to defend myself. Now that was devastating! I would often allow the anger I felt to fester and turn to bitterness and resentment. I was angry because I couldn't say what I wanted to say and do what I wanted to do, which was to lay hands on them, and I don't mean in the holy Christian way either. I wanted them to feel the pain I was feeling, like the recipient of the harsh words they had just spewed out toward me.

As a teenager, I remember being called in front of the church and told that I had a bad attitude, probably for something I said or didn't agree with. For years after that, I felt that I had been labeled "the girl with a bad attitude." Since I didn't want to disappoint, I tried to live up to it so people would learn not to mess with me and say whatever they wanted to.

It is sometimes very difficult to recover from harsh words. I have heard many stories from people saying how things were said to them as a child that they have never been able to break free from. They are taunted by those words years later, and those same words change their lives simply because they internalize the words spoken to and over them.

In scripture, we read where a simple word was spoken and how it changed the atmosphere and the trajectory of a person's or generation's life. However, as powerful as a word spoken to us can be, none is as powerful as the words we speak over our own lives. Henry Ford once said, "Whether you think you can or you think you can't — you're right." This quote demonstrates how your attitude throughout life controls your altitude in life. A word can bring joy or cause misery. Proverbs 18:21 tells us that "the tongue has the power of life and death." Our words have the power to assassinate, not in the literal sense, but they can certainly character assassinate someone and tear their life apart just by speaking the wrong word(s). I know we have all heard our parents tell us, "if you don't have anything good to say, don't say anything at all." If our words are not edifying and building people up, then those words should remain unspoken-even if we are speaking them over ourselves.

Jesus spoke a powerful word to the raging sea in Mark 4, "Peace, be still. And the wind ceased, and there was a great calm" (vs. 38-39). Just as Jesus's words changed the disciple's narrative, so can our words change our life's storyline, our minds, and every endeavor we embark upon. I urge you to speak words in the atmosphere that affirms, builds up, and encourages others. When we speak words of peace and understanding, we prevent the enemy from coming and inserting his ugly head into our situations and relationships. The enemy wants us to tear each other down and speak those negative words he so often whispers in our ears over our lives. Instead of repeating those negative words-and all those lies, speak the powerful words of God's truth. When we continuously speak God's words, they will become a part of our everyday lives. Choose to speak life. It will give us the boldness and confidence to accomplish all that God is instructing us to do.

My Inspiration: Words are free. It's how you use them, that may cost you.
~ **Kushand Wizdom**

HEAVEN SPEAKS TO ME: In scripture, we read how words have power and how life and death are in the power of the tongue. How has knowing this truth helped you to change how you speak about yourself and to others? Recall a time when your or someone else's words hurt the outcome of a situation.

_____
_____
_____
_____
_____
_____
_____
_____
_____
_____
_____
_____

Scripture Reading: Proverbs 13:3; James 3:2-10; Proverbs 15:1; Matthew 12:36-37

PRAYER: Father God, please help me to become more aware of the words that I allow to come out of my mouth. Help my words to edify and build up rather than tear down. Lord, let the words I speak inspire and not destroy. Let me be so careful to speak words in and with love so that those who hear them can be made whole and reconciled to YOU. Amen!

Week Thirty-Nine

Hidden Gems

What's on the inside?

Every good gift and every perfect gift is from above, Coming down from the Father of lights with whom There is no variation or shadow due to change.

James 1:17

Just as we are unique individually-our God-given gifts, talents, and special abilities make us all a beautiful bouquet of authentic vessels. None of us are the same. God, in his infinite wisdom, thought it best to make each one of us different. Aren't you glad he did? Think about it. Wouldn't it be a boring place to live if everybody, everywhere, were identical? The unfortunate part of it all is that so many of us fail to maximize our full potential in life and never fully embrace the things that make us each so wonderfully different. There is so much unutilized and never realized potential in the grave. How tragic is that?

God did not give us gifts without the means and ability to cultivate them, use them and maximize them. When he placed the gifts inside of us, he set a plan in motion so that provisions would be made for each one of us to display our gifts before great men (Proverbs 18:16). We were not given these gifts just for our benefit or for personal gratification. Neither was this done to make us arrogant or proud. He wanted us to be faithful in using our gifts to bless others. He designed us to be known for our God-given gifts so we can bring glory to

His great name and fulfill his master plan for our lives so our faith would be strengthened.

Our gifts will make way for us in our lives if we begin to exercise and walk in our gifting. We will find real fulfillment and purpose. Furthermore, when God imparts his great gifts within us, we don't get to say we don't want to be placed before great men; it's automatic. Your recognition comes with your gifting. You won't ever have to look for it, beg for it, or manipulate your way into being recognized. When we're gifted, in God's perfect timing, our gift will be exalted when we exalt the gift-giver.

For all the education that we obtain, it is not our academic successes that will make room for us; it is our God-given gifts. So many are consumed with academic accomplishments that they leave their God-given gifts lying dormant, so they never really experience the contentment that comes along with operating out of what God has so freely given to them. Don't get me wrong, I believe in education. It is so necessary. However, if you're super educated and intelligent but aren't exercising your gifts, you'll probably find yourself struggling at some point in life.

If you're educated but haven't tapped into your talent, you're most likely going to be unfulfilled and empty, always feeling like something is missing; because it is. Our gifts are the key to our success. All the hidden gems we have allowed to remain dormant and collect mounds of dust are what's keeping us from a life of contentment. You may even wonder, "If I have all these gems and gifts inside, why did they reject me." Perhaps it's because God hid your value from your rejecters. After all, they were not assigned to your destiny. So be very glad and move on but don't you dare give up. If you can't excel with talent, at least allow yourself to triumph with effort. Just don't stop.

Not only were our gifts designed to make room for us, but they are to bring us before great men! We are sitting on loaded treasure boxes that could be taking us to the next level. Realizing our hidden gifts and talents could also be the catalyst God uses to bring us financial stability. Discovering your gift and using it will make you a commodity. You won't ever have to beg someone to let you come and sing or play your instrument or whatever it is that you do well. No matter what continent you travel to, there will always be a place for you in it once you discover and manifest your gift. Even David used his talent playing his harp for Saul when the evil spirit had come upon him, and scripture said that Saul was refreshed and was well, and the evil spirit departed from him (1 Samuel 16:23).

The journey of discovery can be quite adventurous if you don't already know what your gifts are. Seeking the God of every good and perfect gift is how you will realize what you are supposed to do in this life. Be intentional about finding your gifts. Don't allow life to come and go, and all your talents are buried with you. There is a world that is waiting to be blessed by your gift, and needing to be encouraged by your talents. Permit your gifts to come out of hiding and be alive and thrive. Use what God has given you to bring Him glory and to fulfill your God-designed purpose on earth. Our purpose and our giftings go hand in hand, always working in sync to bring harmony to our lives.

My Inspiration: There's power in allowing yourself to be known and heard, in owning your unique story, in using your authentic voice
~ **Michelle Obama**

HEAVEN SPEAKS TO ME: Have you discovered what your gifts are? What hidden gems have you discovered or are currently discovering inside of you? Explain what your journey of discovery has been like and what it has meant to your Christian walk.

_____
_____
_____
_____
_____
_____
_____
_____
_____
_____
_____

Scripture Reading: 1 Peter 4:10; Romans 12:6-8; 1 Corinthians 12:6-11; Exodus 35:10; Colossians 3:23-24

PRAYER: Precious God of all creation, I thank you for creating me in your wonderful image. I am so grateful that you made me creative, inventive, and innovative. May I always use my creativity to bring you and your creation glory and joy. Father, let your creativity flow through me so that everything that I bring about will bring a smile to your beautiful face and that your great name will be praised and always lifted high. Amen!

Week Forty

Dare to Be Different

◆◆◆◆◆◆◆◆◆

But my servant Caleb has a different attitude than the others have. He has remained loyal to me, so I will bring him into the land he explored. His descendants will possess their full share of that land.

Numbers 14:24 (NLT)

Despite popular belief, being different is not a bad thing. Many highly successful people are "different." Sometimes that's exactly what it takes to get to where we need to be in life. I read a book once titled "I Dare You!" by William. H. Danforth, the founder of Ralston Purina, which is now owned by Nestlé. In the book, Danforth challenges others to do more than just be average or normal-whatever that is. The ideas he provided were simplistic and could be applied to anyone's life. It is specifically for the daring few who are headed somewhere special in life. He encouraged his readers to set goals for whatever they want, work hard to meet those goals, and maintain a well-balanced life. Then, he says, "You will have lived a life that matters." He further states that we must push ourselves to not do less than we are capable of doing. This only makes us mediocre. Be courageous and bold in whatever you set out to do, and go beyond the norm.

Now, there may be some hits and a whole lot of misses, but I am convinced that while those hits may ultimately get us to our destiny, it's the misses that build our character. If I had allowed myself to always focus on the misses and never hope for the hits, I would have counted myself out a long time ago. I can't count the number of misses I've had in my life and continue to have. But the Word of God delivers some really good news about the blessings in store for people who have the right attitude and a humbled spirit.

Take Caleb, for instance. Regardless of how all the other spies saw things, he decided to be a non-conformist and be different and go against the grain. He didn't allow his desire to be popular to overshadow his need to be different and passionate about the things of God. Everyone wants to fit in somewhere, right? But at what cost are you willing to forfeit your promised land just to be a part of the Jones clan, the housewives of Houston, or Cypress, or Atlanta, or whichever clan, click, or group the enemy has convinced you to connect yourself with this month.

Beware of those individuals whose perspectives have been seared with a hot iron and are no longer able to differentiate the voice of God from man. For Caleb's eyes to see what he saw, he had to have God's divine perspective in mind. If he had allowed his vision to be blurred by what was happening around him, he would have seen the same giants that the others saw. But instead, he saw beyond the enemy's army to what God had promised. He saw a land flowing with milk and honey and freedom, not a life of confusion, lost direction, and captivity.

When God makes us a promise, we can stand on it! It matters not what storms or giants or stock market crashes are going on at the moment; we can look confidently at the wars happening around us and the enemies that are closing in on every side and **still** see the promised land that God has provided for those who have chosen to believe his report.

People may look at you strangely and call you crazy, but it shouldn't matter. Daring to be different is being insistent on trusting God anyhow. Don't be scared to stand out and be different, be afraid of being the same as everyone else. If everybody else is doing what is right in their own eyes and living for only material gain, then we need to live for Christ. If others are being wicked and rebelling, then we ought to live righteously. So go ahead and tread confidently against the grain while others are running scared and retreating. You just keep pressing on, knowing that with every step you take forward in Jesus's name, you are getting closer and closer to the promise. Don't give up. Eventually, you will possess the land!

My Inspiration: The first step to becoming what God made you to be is to stop worrying about what others want you to be.
~ Rick Warren

HEAVEN SPEAKS TO ME: What insurmountable obstacles have you had in your life that made you want to retreat and turn back? Maybe you didn't feel like a grasshopper, but you felt like something else. Explain that experience and how your reaction to it made you different and set you apart from others who had similar experiences.

_____

_____

_____

_____

_____

_____

_____

_____

_____

_____

Scripture Reading: Romans 12:6-8; 1 Peter 4:10-11; Ephesians 2:10; 1 Peter 2:9; Psalms 139:13-14; Jeremiah 1:5

PRAYER: Father in heaven, for months now, it seems like the circumstances in my life are insurmountable. It seems the enemy has surrounded me and is taunting me. But as I walk this Christian walk, help me to see from your divine perspective. I don't want to see giants overtaking me. I want to envision myself possessing the land that you promised me. Help me not to be overcome with fear but rather let my faith be much greater than my fears. Amen!

Week Forty-One

Moments That Matter

*You don't know what will happen tomorrow.
Your life Is like a fog. You can see it for a
short time, but then It goes away.*

James 4:14 (ERV)

If we have learned nothing else in the past two years, we know now more than ever that every single moment we have above ground matters. Years ago, there was a saying, "Here today and gone tomorrow." Well, we can no longer say that because it's no longer true. The truth now is, here today and gone today. Gone are the days when we sit around and "chew the fat," so to speak, and waste time as if we had plenty to spare. Moments are no longer perpetual and plenteous in number but rather sparse and very limited. For this reason, they should be cherished and well-guarded, not wasted.

Each moment we spend arguing with our loved ones over something that doesn't amount to anything that matters. The time we spend working ourselves into frenzy matters. Whether we over-cooked our loved one's favorite meal or took time out of our day to stand in agreement with a friend or colleague, it all matters. We must be intentional about each moment God gives us so that we are careful not to squander them away with the distractions of the day.

In those rare instances when we get to experience the wonderful moments in life, it should cause our hearts to be filled with joy and flutter with praise and adoration to God. Rest assured that difficult moments are lurking around the corner. They are sure to come and invade our lives at some point, but we must remember that they come to cause us to seek God all the more. Even when we go through periods when our mere existence becomes mundane, and it seems like we are stuck in the rut of life, we can still sit back and remember the goodness of God down through the years.

Our sweet and precious moments should always include time spent with God in prayer and devotion. We can't allow ourselves to become so busy working for God that we neglect to spend time with God. Each time we spend time in his presence, he makes us new. Every moment of every day is valuable because it brings a fresh beginning and new mercies that we haven't experienced before.

So often, we rush through everything while living with nothing. Our lives should be lived on and with purpose. It should be lived with God-given peace and gratitude for the life we have been so graciously granted. We need to live in those moments our Father has given to us and not worry about what we are not able to change, like our future. Living in the present moment is to let go of the past and not wait for the future. Just live. Live the lives God has given us. Live consciously with an awareness that each moment is indeed a gift that not all are granted.

How does one live in the moment? Maintaining a fully focused life entails being mentally present and involved in what we are experiencing. Concentrating on the now, one moment at a time. Pay attention to the small things and be aware of our surroundings. Perform random acts of kindness. I promise it will make the moment so much sweeter.

Don't wait for tomorrow, live today because time waits for no man and the night goes quickly. Embrace the present moment. It is just a vapor.

Here one moment and gone the next.

My Inspiration: The only limit to our realization of tomorrow will be our doubts of today.
~ Franklin D. Roosevelt

HEAVEN SPEAKS TO ME: How do you view your life? What practices do you have in place in your life that allows you to pause and take in the present moment? In what ways do you appreciate your time with friends and family? How do you cherish your time with God?

_____
_____
_____
_____
_____
_____
_____
_____
_____
_____

Scripture Reading: 2 Corinthians 4:16-17' Matthew 12:36-37; Proverbs 15:1; Matthew 6:33-34

PRAYER: Father God, I know my life is just a vapor, but I so appreciate the time you have given me. Time to know and appreciate You for who You are. Time to spend with family and friends building sweet and precious memories. Help me not to squander my time by indulging in frivolous things that amount to nothing. Let me not waste time arguing and burning bridges that I might have to cross over again. Let me live out my days cherishing every moment and bringing glory and honor to your wonderful name. Amen!

Week Forty-Two

The Anchor That Holds

He is the Rock; his work is perfect: for all his ways are judgement: a God of truth and without iniquity, just and right is he.

Deuteronomy 32:4

When I watched the movie Titanic, I enjoyed it. However, I remember thinking, "gee, this is a very long movie," but still, I couldn't or wouldn't stop watching because I was intrigued by it. The costumes, the special effects, the acting! It was all great. Every award the movie and its actors received was well deserved. However, I just couldn't quite wrap my mind around how something so grandiose could sink the way that it did. The captain and all those on it had so much faith in its ability to carry them and get them safely to their destinations. They even dubbed it the "unsinkable ship." It was the largest, most luxurious ocean voyager of its time. Their faith in this great water vessel would become shaky in the soon-to-be troubled waters of the North Atlantic Ocean. The passengers' confidence in the ocean liner would soon fail as well as the captains' ability to keep it afloat. You see, the ship had crashed into a large iceberg in the wee hours of the morning on April 15, 1912, sending the ship and 1,500 of its passengers mercilessly deep within the ocean. It was simply hard to watch toward the end. I may have even cried. It was sad.

As horrific as the sinking of the Titanic was, there are still so many unanswered questions about how and why it sank all these years later. There's been much speculation, but the truth of the matter is we may not ever find the truth. Was there any way this catastrophe could have been mitigated? Could the anchor have played a role in saving the Titanic or its passengers? The answer is no. The waters that the Titanic sank in were said to be over 2 miles deep. The anchor's chain would not have been nearly long enough despite it reportedly weighing an incredible 15 tons.

I was amazed when I learned the actual size of that anchor and how it still wasn't able to prevent the catastrophic events of that dreadful morning. I don't know for sure if they ever attempted to drop it as one measure of mitigation, but it may not have even helped if they did. How often have we built our lives around something or someone that we thought would be an added layer of protection and security for us? At some point in our lives, we all become anchored to something; our investments, education, bank accounts, retirement, and even our prestige for those of us who were fortunate enough to obtain it. But how confident are you in what you think is holding you?

Though anchors are built to hold a craft in place, they only work if they are aligned properly to something firm, deep and strong. If you find yourself surrounded by what feels like quicksand and you're being sucked into a lifestyle that you know is not what God intended for you, then you need to be sure that you are holding on to something strong enough to pull you up and out of your sinking sand. That something is Jesus. Take hold of his righteous right hand and allow him to pull you out of the muck and mire to your wealthy place. You wouldn't attach your yacht to a stuffed teddy bear, would you? Lord no! You would grip it to something strong and sturdy and with a solid foundation. But isn't that what happens when we anchor ourselves to worldly things and people? We attach our lives to things and people with artificial strength, counterfeit promises, and no real power to save us. When the torrential rains hit you hard, trust nothing and no one but God to deliver you. He is the one true constant and reliable being in our lives. We must stand strong in our faith, constantly reminding ourselves that having a shipwrecked faith will never get us to shore. Having a steadfast hope in the living God will (1 Timothy 4:10).

When you make Jesus your anchor, you have abounding hope (Romans 15:13). Not every once in a while, or occasionally or when we fill like having it. No. God says He wants us to abound in hope through the power of the Holy Spirit. Is what you are anchored to stronger than what you are going through? Though we may experience turbulence, and while the winds blow, the rain will still fall, and the waters around us will be troubled, we can remain confident that our anchor will hold because it's' gripped by the Solid Rock called Jesus!

Let the words of this song always keep you in remembrance of the only One who is our firm foundation, our Solid Rock.

In Times Like These

"In times like these, you need a
Savior In times like these, you need
an anchor Be very sure. Be very
sure, that your anchor holds and
grips the Solid Rock, This Rock is
Jesus. Yes He's the One This Rock is
Jesus, the only One
Be very sure, be very sure that your
Anchor holds and grips the Solid Rock!

My Inspiration: When we feel the stress of the storm, we learn the strength of the ANCHOR.

~ Deborah Ann

HEAVEN SPEAKS TO ME: Do an assessment of your life. When the trials of life hit you hard, what or who are you most anchored to? Be honest. Has God always been the first place you have looked to for help, or was He the last resort when all else failed? How has reading this devotion helped you become more anchored in Him?

_____
_____
_____
_____
_____
_____
_____
_____
_____
_____
_____

Scripture Reading: Hebrews 6:19, Acts 27:30-40, Romans 5:5, Psalms 62:5-6

PRAYER: Strong and mighty God, thank you for being my anchor, my rock. Lord, I am so grateful that You are strong enough to hold all my current issues and concerns, fears for my future, and the tears of my past. You are what holds me and my loved ones together when life starts to drift us out to a deep, dark sea and pull us under. Thank you for securing me and for being the solid rock on which I stand. Amen!

Week Forty-Three

Flawed With Purpose

But I have raised you up for this very purpose, that I might show you my power and that my name might be proclaimed in all the earth.

Exodus 9:16

Back in the day, I almost became a diamontologist. By now, I was working at my second jewelry store, Kay Jewelers being my first, and the manager wanted me to study to take the certification exam. He almost sold me on it, but I just couldn't see myself making a career out of it, and outside of that, there was no need for me to have it. I just figured I would know what I knew, and there was no point in going through the motions of studying if I was never going to use any of it. So, I decided to take a pass on the offer.

I did learn a few things during my time in the jewelry business though. One of them is the fact that just because a diamond had flaws didn't mean that it lost its value or that it didn't still have its ability to shine. Their purpose and worth remain even with the imperfections because when given, the emotions they bring with them, especially coming from someone with a sincere heart, can make up for their less-than-perfect qualities.

Did you know that diamonds, like people, also have birthmarks? In the world of diamonds, these birthmarks are considered imperfections or inclusions. They are formed under the conditions of intense heat and pressure within the earth's crust.

These inclusions cause the diamond to be unique and one of a kind because none of them are completely identical. There are many diamond inclusion types, and most, if not all, diamonds will have at least one inclusion (except for the rare flawless ones). While some inclusions are clearly visible to the naked eye, most of them are not, and for those, we would examine with a loupe, a small handle-less magnifying device used to see small details more closely.

Now I have to tell you that in the jewelry industry, the more inclusions a diamond has, the cheaper it tends to be, and vice versa. The fewer imperfections, the clearer it's likely to be, hence the inflated price tag. I could go on and on about different kinds of flaws and imperfections a diamond could have, but, the point I want to make is regardless of their flaws and imperfections, size, or shape, they all have value.

The purpose of a man giving a diamond to his beloved woman is to symbolize his love and covenant with her in the marriage. Because of his love, her flaws, whether visible or not, are not reflected in the diamond he gives. So it is with our Heavenly Father. When we accept Him as our Lord and Savior, He does not choose who He will bless with the most stuff based on the number of flaws we have. In Acts 10:34, we read that God is no respecter of persons: But in every nation, he that feareth him, and worketh righteousness, is accepted with him.

Aren't you thankful that despite our shortcomings and imperfections, God still gave us purpose and saw us as people worth dying for? Our flaws do not diminish our value in God's eyes. He uses whoever has a willing and surrendered heart toward Him. Only He can see our imperfections as an opportunity to get more glory. An opportunity to show the world just how great He is. And, to use our imperfections as a reminder to the world that what they chose to discard as useless and deemed unworthy, He had already designed a perfect plan and given a divine purpose so that no man has the power to devalue and throw us away.

Bring all your scars and imperfections to the throne of grace and lay them at the feet of Jesus. Allow the Father to turn your flaws into purpose and use it to bring glory to His name. Permit Him to cover them, not as to hide them from the world, but to beautify them and make you shine so the world can marvel at the mighty works of the master's hands!

My Inspiration: We won't be distracted by comparison if we are captivated by purpose.
~ **Bob Goff**

HEAVEN SPEAKS TO ME: Share what you believe to be your purpose. Write about the moment your purpose became clear to you and how it made you feel. In what ways are you living out your purpose each day? If you are unsure of your purpose, in what ways are you seeking for it to be revealed to you?

_____
_____
_____
_____
_____
_____
_____
_____
_____
_____
_____
_____

Scripture Reading: Job 42:2; Proverbs 19:21, Proverbs 20:5; Ephesians 1:11; 2 Timothy 1:9

PRAYER: Heavenly Father, I pray that I may fulfill the work that you have purposed for me to do in this life. May I complete every assignment given to me in a way that pleases you and without complaint? I know my life is not my own; it is yours to work through me. Help me to understand my purpose fully., I am so grateful for this life you've so graciously given me and have blessed me to live out thus far. Let me shine like the diamond You created me to be. Amen!

Week Forty-Four

Providential Compass

◆◆◆◆◆◆◆◆◆◆◆

Indeed, forty years You provided for them in the wilderness and they were not in want; their clothes did not wear out, nor did their feet swell

Nehemiah 9:21

Being lost is not a good feeling for me. It's a feeling of utter frustration and even a little scary at times, depending on where I'm at. Talking about a complete waste of valuable time and energy circling back and forth in an attempt to navigate your way back to sanity. Precious time has gone down the drain as I try to finesse my way through the maze of unfamiliar territories and less traveled roads. Yet, even with the potential of getting lost, I am not the least bit deterred from packing my bags, hopping in my wheels, and zooming off for a road trip. Why? Because somehow, before I set out, I feel confident that even if I do get turned around, I will not be lost forever. Some way, and at some point, I know I will find my way home safely.

Think about what a compass is and does for those needing direction. A compass is a symbol of safety and protection. It can protect us from getting lost, and just in case we do, it guides us homeward. In modern-day, it might be likened to a navigation system, instructing us to turn left on Nowhereville Dr. in 1.4 miles, then keep straight for 0.6 miles, then take a right on Mainstream Blvd, and a slight left on Almost There Ave. in 2.8 miles. Before long, you are getting a message letting you know you have arrived at your destination.

When the compass was created, it is said to have changed the world by making it possible for explorers to sail far out into the oceans regardless of what the weather was like. This led to more explorations and discoveries. The same is true when we put our confidence and faith in the providential compass of the Holy Spirit, who leads and guides. With it, we can walk on water without fear of going under. It enables us to venture out into the deep, knowing that as long as we have the presence of the Holy Spirit with us, we will not be overtaken by the tides, and should we decide to travel in the darkest of the world, we won't be lost in the wilderness. We can rest assured that it will guide us through, over, and around the rough terrains of life, especially during times of confusion when we have lost our way. It helps align us to our values and spiritual truths that will guide our actions when we feel life it has been unfair.

Take the Israelites, for example. They should have made it to the Promised Land in days, not decades. However, despite the errors in their ways, the murmuring and complaining, and the rebellion, God still aided them in the wilderness experience. The Lord instructed them to wage war against the Canaanites. For them to carry this commandment out would require an act of determined obedience on their part. It would prove whose side they were on and whom their faith was in. Instead, the Israelites rebelled against God 7 times. They complained about shortages, worshipped a golden calf, fought the Amalekites, sent spies into Canaan, then complained that the land was unconquerable, and so on. Upon hearing the spies' fearful report concerning the conditions in Canaan, the Israelites refused to take possession of it. Because of their discontentment, God decreed that the Israelites would wander in the wilderness for 40 years due to their unwillingness to take the land. God condemns them to death in the wilderness until a new generation can grow up and carry out the task.

When we operate under the providential compass of the Holy Spirit, it releases God's providence in our lives. In God's providence, there is provision, protection, peace, and promise. God goes beyond our existence and is already at our end. His providence and divine care even go as far as counting the number of hairs on our heads.

His providence activates his provision for us. Conversely, if we disobey His commands and live outside of his divine providence, we will be separated and remain captives to our sins. We will be like the Israelites wandering, blinded by the allures of Satan as if we have no compass to lead us back to God. Let the providence of the Holy Spirit be your compass today.

My Inspiration: A firm faith in the universal providence of God is the solution of all earthly troubles.

~ B.B. Warfield

HEAVEN SPEAKS TO ME: In times when you were lost and confused, what was your source of direction? What was it that gave you a sense of protection? And, how would you explain the providence of God working in your life today?

_____

_____

_____

_____

_____

_____

_____

_____

_____

_____

Scripture Reading: Psalm 22:28; Exodus 19:4; Romans 11:36; 1 Chronicles 29:11; Psalm 103:19

PRAYER: Father in heaven, thank you for being omnipotent, omniscient, and omnipresent. Your sovereignty is unmatched, for you are the God over all things. Dear Lord, I am so grateful for your provision, protection, and guidance in my life. No matter where this life leads me, I know without a doubt that the providence of your Holy Spirit covers me and shields me from all hurt, harm, and danger. Mere words are not enough to say thank you. Amen!

Week Forty-Five

Flashy Dashes

◆◆◆◆◆◆◆◆◆

Set your affections on things above and not on things of this earth. ³For ye are dead, and your life is hid with Christ in God

Colossians 3:2-3

O*nce upon a time, why back when, I wanted to be in the field of fashion production. I sought out information about FIDM, the Fashion Institute of Design and Merchandising in California. I had gotten the brochures and perused their website to gain all the knowledge I could about attending. I had it all mapped out for myself. Flashy fashions and long flawless legs dawning the runway of a grand production that I had put together was what I envisioned. Although these aspirations were short-lived, I believed that was what I wanted at that time.*

I attended a funeral once some years back. The individual who gave the eulogy spoke about "What's in Your Dash." The moral of the message was about what we do with our lives from the time we are born to the time we die. The period from our born date to our death date is our dash. Now, I have seen people do all manner of things with their dash, including myself. We have all lived life dangerously and on edge at times. Some were a little more responsible and tried to do some good, making a difference where they could. Then there are those who like to live vicariously through others. They loved the glitz, blitz, dings, and blings of life. Anything and anyone that allowed them to be flashy and in the limelight they loved. They wanted to live the life of a celebrity. They would make it a point to be where the action was and where everybody was somebody. As a result, they found themselves living far above their means, drowning in debt and living up to a standard that they just couldn't maintain. They were consumed with the idea of being wealthy and lived erroneously believing that if they just had more, they would be liked and maybe even loved more.

How tragic it is to live a life where you are not permitted to be your authentic self! A life that only allowed you to live comparing yourself to someone else, coveting what others have. Operating in your giftings and being confident in who and how God made you render a certain kind of freedom and peace that you can't get anywhere else. When you know without a doubt that you are living your life as God, the creator intended, giving nothing and no one more attention than you give to Him, you will no longer feel the need to look with envy at what others have that you might not. You can trust and believe God for what you want and know in your heart that if it's His will, you will have it (Matthew 6:33).

So how do we set our minds on eternal things and turn our attention from the glitz and blitz of this world? Be intentional. Serve God on purpose and with purpose. Constantly feed your mind with the word and works of God. Continuously examine your thought life (2 Corinthians 10:5). Leave your old self, ways, and habits behind (2 Corinthians 5:17). Choose to follow God's leading (Proverbs 3:5-6). Thank God for what he has already given you. Spend time with like-minded believers. And, most importantly, spend plenty of time with God in your secret place, drawing nigh to Him and not the temporal things of this world (James 4:8).

Use the time God has blessed you to live on this earth, bringing glory to Him. Utilize your time wisely to make a difference in someone's life, in your church, your workplace, in your home, and in the lives of your family. Don't spend your dash chasing phantom dreams that God never intended for your life. Look at your own life and not somebody else's, and make the most out of it. Live it to the fullest so that when your dash is sealed off and comes to an end, it will be exemplary of a life well lived in Christ Jesus.

My Inspiration: You only live once, but if you do it right, once is enough
~ **Mae West**

HEAVEN SPEAKS TO ME: What areas, outside of time spent with God, have you focused on too much? In what ways have you learned to set your affections on heavenly things and not the things of this world? Have you ever wanted something the world was offering that you knew was contrary to God's word?

_____
_____
_____
_____
_____
_____
_____
_____
_____
_____
_____
_____

Scripture Reading: Philippians 4:8; Romans 12:2; Psalms 94:9; James 4:7

PRAYER: Heavenly Father, the world is always flashing its glitz and bling in front of me. Often I have been tempted to chase after it even though I know it's not your will for my life. Lord, help me to be strong in my faith and walk in the truth that everything I need is in a life spent with you. Increase my desire to live through you, rise with you and rejoice because of you. Amen!

Week Forty-Six

A Doubt-Filled Mind

*When doubts filled my mind, your comfort gave
me renewed hope and cheer.*

Psalms 94:19 (NLT)

There were so many times when I allowed doubt to diminish the hope that I once had inside. It had been brought on by one failure after another. A single disappointment, then two or three. Back-to-back rejections. Setback and let-down felt like the norm, and before long, so was doubt. I developed an attitude of doubt without even realizing it. Every thought seemed to be accompanied by a doubt-filled rationale that led me to believe something probably would not work out simply because that was the "norm."

I had grown accustomed to a life where nothing exciting happened. It was a very dull existence of hum-drum days filled with very little to no sunshine, only storm clouds, and rain.

One day I began to reminisce on a time when nothing seemed impossible. I was fearless and determined. I wore confidence like a badge of honor. So what happened? What hindered me? Had something spooked me into thinking that whatever I pursued was no longer attainable? What had my spirit so discouraged and afraid to try again?

Then, it hit me like a rock! I had simply stopped remembering the times God had brought me through before. I realized that I only doubted God when I forgot what he had already done for me. I had stopped believing that what God had for me is just for me. When I allowed myself to believe again there was no need for me to fear being told no, or "we chose someone else for the position," or whatever it may be. If the answer was no, then it wasn't for me, and not because I let doubt fill my mind to the point of not believing.

When we feel anxious about a decision, we need to ask God to help us experience his divine peace and find ways to remind ourselves that God is in full control, not us. Isn't it exhausting letting fear and doubt control our minds? Aren't you ready for God to do a new thing in your life? I know I certainly am. At some point, we must realize that there are just simply some things in life that we cannot control. If we don't want fear to control our lives and we know for sure that we don't have control, then why don't we just take a step back, get out of our way and release full control back to where it belongs with God?

Continuing to attempt to wrap our short arms around things that we were never designed to embrace is absolute foolishness at its finest. It doesn't matter how long we may think our arms are they will never be long enough to wrap them around the uncertainties of an uncertain tomorrow.

Spend time reading and studying God's word to obtain peace and instruction in every situation. Replace doubt with faith in the God *who is able to do exceedingly abundantly all that we can ask or think according to the power that works in us* (Ephesians 3:20).

When we have no guarantees that our plans will work, we go into panic mode and become fearful, and start worrying. This is not of God. He does not give us this kind of spirit but one of love and soundness of mind (2 Timothy 1:7). God is neither fearful nor frugal so whatever we need, no matter how big, trust God to deliver. Run the doubt right out of your mind, and instead fill your mind with the word and his promise that assures us that "all things are possible to him who believes" (Mark 9:23). Command those negative doubt-filled thoughts to vacate the premises of your mind so you can stand firmly on the word of God.

My Inspiration: The only limit to our realization of tomorrow will be our doubts of today
~ Franklin D. Roosevelt

HEAVEN SPEAKS TO ME: There are so many things to make us doubt. In what ways have you learned to replace doubt with faith? What scripture(s) have you studied lately to help you combat the doubt that wants to fill your mind? How have you applied it to the decisions you are faced with?

_____
_____
_____
_____
_____
_____
_____
_____
_____
_____
_____
_____
_____

Scripture Reading: Psalms 32:8; Romans 14:23; James 1:6; Matthew 21:21; John 20:27;

PRAYER: Thank you, Jesus, for breaking through my doors of doubt and unbelief. Lord, I believe but help my unbelief. I am grateful that You are active and present in my life, even when I cannot see You, even when in my sin and I rejected You. Regardless of my doubt-filled mind, you still love me. Thank you for speaking to me through Your word to give me direction and peace. Amen!

Week Forty-Seven

Supernatural Downpours

For as the rain cometh down, and the snow from heaven, and returneth not thither, but watereth the earth, and maketh it bring forth and bud, that it may give seed to the sower, and bread to the eater.

Isaiah 55:10

I'm certain you've seen the movies and TV commercials where the kid pretends to be a superhero. They put on their makeshift capes, and away they go to solve world peace as they know and understand it. Or the Sci-Fi films where the paranormal tries to take control and terrorize the nation and becomes the nemesis or the neighborhood villain. Though that is all make-believe, many taboos have developed around the idea of the "supernatural." Some people think the whole subject is rather eerie and downright spooky. But, as Christians, we believe in God's supernatural work and understand that those unexplainable happenings keep our faith and hope alive and strong.

The Bible uses many supernatural symbols to illustrate God's favor on his people. Rain, for instance, was one of the most significant signs. However, the absence of it meant God's wrath had come upon them. On the contrary, the abundance of it was symbolic that the curse was over. The blessings would soon follow and begin pouring once again. So what is a supernatural downpour, and why should we want it? It is about, or being, or beyond what is natural, unexplainable by natural law or phenomena, abnormal. Now, we as Christians know that our God will supply all our needs according to his riches in glory by Christ Jesus (Philippians 4:19). But what does that supply entail? 1 John 5:14-15 tells us that we can be confident in knowing that whenever we ask anything according to his will, he hears us. Therefore, if we know this for sure because he is not a God that he should lie (Numbers 23:19), whatever we ask, we ought to know without a doubt that we have it.

That all sounds good and simple enough, right? Well, there are times when our circumstances are so dire, and we have run completely out of our finite options, and it's just simply not humanly possible to get us out of the messes we find ourselves in. But God is a God of impossible situations. Getting us out of tight spots and painful predicaments is his specialty. Sometimes we need a supernatural miracle! Something that no one else can do but God so that no one else but God can get all the glory.

How did God provide for the children of Israel for 40 years in the wilderness? No one's clothing wore out; they had manna from heaven every day to sustain them. Then there was that day when two fish and five barley loaves of bread fed 5,000! This event is known as the "miracle of the five loaves and two fish," and it occurred on two separate occasions. The first time he fed 5,000 (Matt. 14:15-21). The second he fed 4,000 (Matt. 15:32-39). These supernatural downpours were not by happenstance. They were the manifestation of the Trinity working together to perform what mortal man never could, miracles from on high.

Your supernatural downpour may appear to be light-years away. You may very well be in the needy stage of life where nothing seems to be going your way, and you need God to work in your life, your circumstances, your finances, and your relationships like never before. You don't need just one blessing or one day of good fortune. You are in dire need of a supernatural downpour! I am here to tell you that supernatural downpours still happen, and if that's what you need, then ask God for it knowing that he will bring it to pass and supply everything that's needed; when you need it. Seek God for the latter rain. Don't just seek him for the stuff; seek for a downpouring of more and more of Him. Let his grace and presence overtake you and fill you with his supernatural strength and power to ask whatever you will and believe it is so!

My Inspiration: The fool is thirsty in the midst of a downpour.
~ **Ethiopian Proverb**

HEAVEN SPEAKS TO ME: *Ever been in dire need of anything? Describe how God answered your prayer(s) with a supernatural downpour and how all of your needs were met. How did that experience change your walk with Christ?*

_____
_____
_____
_____
_____
_____
_____
_____
_____
_____
_____
_____
_____
_____
_____
_____

Scripture Reading: Jeremiah 14:22, 32:27; Genesis 7:17; Job 37:6; Habakkuk 3:10

PRAYER: *Jehova Jireh, your Holy word tells me that You are no respect of persons. Lord, when I need supernatural downpours, give me the unwavering faith to believe that you will also provide everything I need when I need it, just as I've seen you do for so many others. Help me to rest in your ability to perform the supernatural in every area of my life. Amen!*

Week Forty-Eight

Something Within

◆◆◆◆◆◆◆◆◆◆

Don't you know that you yourselves are God's temple and that God's Spirit dwells in your midst?

1 Corinthians 3:16

I have an astonishing confession to make. I'm not a perfect Christian. If the truth is told, sometimes I just don't feel saintly or righteous, or good or saved even. There have been days and seasons in my life when I didn't want to read the scriptures, pray or attend worship services. I simply didn't want to be bothered. I wanted to be left alone to waddle and wade in the troubled waters of my deep despair-and I wanted to do it in peace without someone quoting scriptures and telling me all the reasons why I shouldn't feel the way I was feeling.

Everything about God and church seemed to be a tedious chore. Whenever I would try to read the word or pray, my mind would just flood like a rushing waterfall of distractions. When I would read, I would skip around the scriptures, never really settling long enough to put my roots down and study them.

Then there were times when I just wanted a quick fix. Nothing that really satisfied but only what would pacify me long enough to get through whatever I was going through. I looked for easy encouragement. I searched for the "feeling" I got from hearing God's word, but the thing is, I wanted the feeling I got from Him more than I wanted Him.

Even though I knew that was a terrible place to be in, somehow, I would end up there repeatedly until I came to the end of myself. Until something within my soul decided to arise and fight back with the strength given to me by the One who created me and promised that if I did it through and with Him, I could do anything. I have found, no matter whether I felt like reading it or not, the best way to combat spiritual apathy is by immersing myself in the Word and works of God. By continuing to go back for more and more. By not allowing ourselves to become anxious and distracted, we can become more focused on scripture and meditate on it so that it can truly speak to us. So it can become rooted deep within our souls.

When we allow the Holy Spirit to take over and permit Jesus to have Lordship in our lives, no matter where we are, how we feel, or what negative words our ears may hear, there will always be something within us to cause us to stand when we don't feel we have the strength to do so. Something within us will cause us to press forward despite feeling pressed down. It will enable us to keep looking ahead even though our past is following close behind us. And it will make us continue running the race that God has given us regardless of having the wind knocked out of us.

At one point in my life, I heard hymns all the time. I attended an AME church that my aunt Gin pastored. My aunt Esther (Babe is what she was so affectionately called) played the piano, and she would often sing a hymn called "Something Within." I tried to remember the words but could only recall the stanza that held the title of the song. So, I looked up the words, and still, they blessed me.

> Preachers and teachers would make their appeal,
> Fighting as soldiers on great battlefields;
> When to their pleadings my poor heart did yield,
> All I can say, there is something within

Something within me that holdeth the reins;
Something within me that banishes pain;
Something within me I cannot explain;
All that I know, there is something within.
Have you that something, that burning desire?
Have you that something, that never doth tire?
Oh, if you have it-that Heavenly Fire!
Then let the world know there is something within

It's interesting that whenever I have searched for myself in the Word, I often feel so doomed. I feel arid and dismayed because I know I didn't measure up to what I was reading. But, when I learned to search for God, not myself, in His Word, I find only His truth about Him, myself, and my situations. When we read about God and who He is in ALL of His wonder and splendor, that is what produces joy within us and hope for brighter days ahead. It gives us the true satisfaction that our arid souls need to finish this race. Then and only then can we march as Christian soldiers in the army of our Heavenly King!

When your spirit gets low and you begin to feel apathetic, remind yourself of that something within. Give the Holy Spirit permission to permeate the inner workings of your soul to uplift you to a place of praise and worship, singing and dancing before the King of Kings.

My Inspiration: There is not in the world a kind of life more sweet and delightful than that of a continual conversation with God; those only can comprehend it who practice and experience it
~ **Brother Lawrence**

HEAVEN SPEAKS TO ME: Describe how it feels knowing that you have the Holy Spirit within you. How has the Holy Spirit helped you get through difficult times? Name a time when spiritual apathy set in, and you had to rely on the "Something Within" to pull you through your arid season.

_____

_____

_____

_____

_____

_____

_____

_____

_____

_____

_____

_____

Scripture Reading: Acts 2:38; John 14:16-17; 2 Timothy 1:14; Acts 5:32

PRAYER: Thank you, Lord God, for your Holy Spirit that comes to comfort, strengthen, and encourage me in my dry seasons and during my valley-low experiences. I can't imagine what I would do if your Spirit did not live on the inside of me to cause me to arise and run this Christian race with grace, hope, and joy. God, help me to always be aware of your presence in my life. Remind me of your goodness so that I will want to keep pressing for the goal no matter how I may feel. Amen!

Week Forty-Nine

Heavens Frequency

My sheep hear my voice, and I know them, and they follow me: ²⁸ And I give unto them eternal life; and they shall never perish, neither shall any man pluck them out of my hand.

John 10:27-28

"Ma'am, can you hear me? Ma'am, ma'am, are you there? I can't hear you; clearly, you're breaking up. There's too much static. Can you hear me, ma'am? Please don't leave me!" Those were the words that were bellowed by a woman in distress on an episode of the series 911. Life was nearly lost because the operator was not able to hear clearly because of a bad connection. How scary is that? You're in dire need of help, and the only one that could help can't hear you because of static and all the other bad connections that keep interfering with the call.

I used to love hearing truck drivers on their CB radios. They'd say, "Breaker, breaker, come in. This is CB calling," and the conversation would begin. Then there were times you could even hear someone else's conversation because the frequency they were using wasn't clear, so it was almost like a party line of sorts, and anyone could jump in.

When I think about that from a spiritual standpoint, how often do we, as believers, allow the static of our chaotic lives to get in the way of our communication with God? We may start good, but then the interference occurs, and before you know it, the distractions have taken over the entire conversation.

Then, when our prayers are not answered when we think they should, we are left to wonder why? Spending undisturbed quality time is what we should strive for every time we go before God in prayer. When we bring all our distractions and worldly static with us in an attempt to reach God's throne room and allow it to impede upon his quality time, instead of blocking it all out to make sure the airways are clear, we limit our access to the heavenly throne room. Our prayers will hit the ceiling and bounce right back at us, leaving us the burden of carrying what we should have been able to cast at the feet of Jesus and leave it there.

We often have no heavenly support because we are too worldly-connected. God's viewpoint is no longer a priority. There's too much static in our airways coming from sources other than the Heavenly Source. When we surrender to the presence of God, we won't have to search for a clear signal; the Holy Spirit will find us right where we are.

Now, there will be times when the agony of our circumstances may stand as a barrier the size of Mount Everest, and getting on Heaven's frequency seems an insurmountable task. It is during this time that we have to press, push, and pull ourselves into the presence of the Almighty to get what we need. In the story of the woman with the issue of blood, the bible tells us that even in her messed up condition and state of mind, she still managed to press and stretch her way to the hem of the garment that would make her well. Though she didn't have the physical strength, she possessed a powerful will to move past the static of the stares and the unwanted comments of those who looked down upon her. It was that will to be on heaven's frequency that made her whole.

When we learn to first seek God's voice, then we will hear God's voice. Our Heavenly Father is constantly speaking to us to lead and guide us in the ways we should go, but we are not always listening. If we discipline ourselves to wait in silence in his presence, being intentional about casting out every negative and disruptive thought, we will find ourselves on Heaven's frequency and will hear all the Father wants to impart to us.

My Inspiration: When it comes to REVELATION, we must properly tune our receiver to heaven's frequency.
~ Larry Y. Wilson

HEAVEN SPEAKS TO ME: What do you do to remove the static in your life? What can you do to ensure that when God is speaking, your lines of communication are open to receive from him?

_____
_____
_____
_____
_____
_____
_____
_____
_____
_____
_____
_____

Scripture Reading: Mark 10:46-52; Isaiah 30:21; Romans 10:17; John 8:47; Isaiah 30:21

PRAYER: Dear Lord, oftentimes when I pray, I am ashamed to say, You don't always have my undivided attention. There's always stuff in the way that prevents me from really entering your throne room. Help me to discipline myself so that when I approach your sacred throne, all else is blocked out, and there's nothing left but me and a loving conversation with my Father. May the static be removed, and your Heavenly frequency is enacted in my life.

Week Fifty

Look To Jesus and Live

If ye then be risen with Christ, seek those things which are above, where Christ sitteth on the right hand of God. ² Set your affections on things above, not things on this earth

Colossians 3:1-2

"Look and live, my brother, live. Look to Jesus now and live...." These were the words to a hymnal I could hear being sung by my Aunt Babe's sweet voice. Her frail aged fingers would be tickling the ivory as best she could, and she would smile and nod her head as she emphatically played each note from memory. Those were memorable days when hymns could be sung and played, and they meant something. Back then, from what my mom told me, they had to learn all stanzas of a hymn. There was no such thing as learning only parts of it and being one and done. Not learning the whole song would mean you miss the meaning, the purpose, and the true intent the writer wanted to convey. In this case, I believe songwriter William Ogden wanted to convey the urgency in what he wrote. He wanted people to hurry up and look to Jesus so they could live. Stop looking around and down but look up to Jesus and live!

The words of this hymn were, in some ways, commands. They instructed us to look and live and to do it now rather than later! I love how this hymn is written. It's line-by-line instructions on how to obtain eternal life and be ecstatic about it! There are so many things in this life that bring us down and cause us to look at any and everything else other than Jesus. In God's love letter to his people, he placed so many promises in it that, if we would just grab hold of them, they would save us, our families, our relationships, our careers, and ultimately our very lives.

Focus on Jesus. Fix your eyes on the eternal God. Looking anywhere else is frugal and will only yield negativity. You'll become preoccupied with things that are irrelevant and not necessary to get you to where God wants you to be. You will be left in a hopeless state of dismay and frustration. Let your gaze be upon Jesus and him alone.

There is no doubt plenty to be down about. If you want to be distressed, look within. If you want to be defeated, then look back at your terrible past and all the mistakes you've made. If you want to be distracted, look around. If you want to be dismayed, then keep looking ahead because no one knows what lies ahead. But, if you need to be delivered, then I encourage you, my friends, to look **up** to Jesus so you can live and live a life filled with his promises and not life's failures. Why? Because his promises are true, yes, and Amen (2 Corinthians 1:20). Allow the words of this hymn to permeate your soul and minister life to your very being.

Look and Live
William A. Ogden (1887)

1 I've a message from the Lord,
Hallelujah! The message unto you I'll give,
'Tis recorded in His Word,
Hallelujah! It is only that you "look and live."

Refrain:
"Look and live," my brother, live.
Look to Jesus now and live.
'Tis recorded in His Word,
Hallelujah! It is only that you
"Look and live."

2 I've a message full of love,
Hallelujah! A message, O my
friend, for you.
'Tis a message from above, Hallelujah!
Jesus said it, and I know 'tis true.
[Refrain]

3 Life is offered unto you. Hallelujah!
Eternal life your soul shall have
If you'll only look to Him. Hallelujah!
Look to Jesus, who alone can save. [Refrain]

4 I will tell you how I came,
Hallelujah! To Jesus when He
made me whole:
'Twas believing in His name, Hallelujah!
I trusted and He saved my soul. [Refrain]

My Inspiration: When you're at your LOWEST, look to the HIGHEST.
~ Unknown

HEAVEN SPEAKS TO ME: Briefly discuss how you have been affected by the things you see and hear around you. In what ways have you learned to block out the negativity and look to Jesus? How has relying on Jesus in tough times made you a better witness?

_____
_____
_____
_____
_____
_____
_____
_____
_____
_____

Scripture Reading: 2 Corinthians 12:10; Psalm 28:7; Psalm 34:5; Hebrews 12:2; Isaiah 40:26:

PRAYER: Heavenly Father, thank You for Your divine guidance. Forgive me for getting beside myself and going ahead of You and Your plans for my life and trying to do things on my own instead of looking to You first. Help me to know when to stop and listen for Your directions. Your ways are perfect. Thank You for offering gentle grace when I look in the wrong direction rather than upward to You. Amen!

Week Fifty-One

Orchestrator of Life

◆◆◆◆◆◆◆◆

I am with you and will watch over you wherever you go, and I will bring you back to this land. I will not leave you until I have done what I have promised you.

Genesis 28:15

Fine art has always intrigued me. Though I am no art connoisseur by any means, I do have an appreciation for it. Some pieces of artwork seem to depict mass confusion. They are simply baffling to look at. You find yourself just staring at it, trying to figure it out. You think, "What in the world was the creator of this piece thinking when they were creating this painted catastrophe?" On the other hand, a real art guru can look at the same piece of work and point out not-so-obvious details that, in their mind, tell a story. I would be scratching my head, thinking aloud, "How did you get all that from looking at that chaos?"

Art sometimes only makes perfect sense in the mind of the creator. As the artist prepares to place the well-thought-out masterpiece in his mind onto the canvas, he strategically places each tool at his disposal; all acrylic paints, each paintbrush, palette, easel, a jar of water, etc. Only the creator can fully understand this process of preparation and inspiration or, in some cases, the method to their madness.

When God created us, we were the product of a divine design, a great masterpiece in the mind of the greatest orchestrator to have ever lived. We were not and are not just a method to his madness. In his perfect image, we were methodically, beautifully, and wonderfully made (Psalm 139:13-14). I know what you are thinking, "there is absolutely nothing perfect about my life." That is a true and correct assessment. Our lives are not perfect, but a perfect God who makes old things like new created us, and that is good enough for me.

Every time we come to a rough season in our lives, the enemy makes us doubt the work of our creator. We begin to live our lives as if God made a mistake in making us the way he did. We attempt to change who we were created to be. We start finding fault with the way our heads are shaped, how stubby our fingers are or how thin our lips are, and how wide our hips are (God has nothing to do with that part, that is all on us).

Though there are some things about our physical appearances that we can change, what God has placed inside is his identifying mark that we are his creation. No one else can take credit for what our creator has placed on the inside of us. He put it there so he could always identify what belongs to him. It does not matter what scars and marks life has left on us; he can still lay claim to what is his.

Nothing in our lives happens by mistake. The orchestrator of our lives has already laid out everything needed to paint each phase on the canvas of our lives. To someone on the outside looking in, our lives may look like a confusing mess right now. Rest assured, the One who has and continues to orchestrate our lives knows exactly the story that will be told once the canvas has been filled with all of his glory.

Each season of our lives is all but a piece of artwork that is being painted by the greatest artist that there ever was. Once done, people will look and stand amazed at the finished product. A canvas once blurred, splashed on, misunderstood, and misinterpreted will be admired by many. Each canvas is overseen by the Curator, who protects and shields us from what will bring us harm and keep us from drawing closer to him. In the end, all will know our lives were divinely orchestrated by the One who directs our hearts to be drawn toward the things and people that will ultimately lead to our destiny.

My Inspiration: Success is remaining faithful to the process God has laid out for you. What God originates, God orchestrates.
~ **Andy Stanley**

HEAVEN SPEAKS TO ME: In which ways have you fully surrendered your plans to God? Discuss a time when you didn't understand the trials you were facing, only to realize that it was all a part of God's master plan for your life to get you to where He wanted you to be.

_____
_____
_____
_____
_____
_____
_____
_____
_____
_____

Scripture Reading: Genesis 45:5-8; Hebrews 13:5; Deuteronomy 7:7-11; Isaiah 45:7; Hebrews 1:1-3

PRAYER: Father God, you have given me so much, but you did not give me the ability to know it all and to know what's best for my life, even though I sometimes think I do. Lord, give me the strength to surrender all to your capable hands, especially when life becomes turbulent. Turn the canvas of my life into one that has relinquished control so that you can freely paint the masterpiece that was divinely designed in the mind of You, the creator and orchestrator of all life. Amen!

Week Fifty-Two

Heaven in My View

And as it is appointed unto men once to die, but after this the judgment.

Hebrews 9:27

Just a few months after relocating to Houston, I accepted a contract assignment as a marketing coordinator to assist a company with its global sales conference in Barcelona, Spain. Since they were pleased with my work, they decided to take me along. It was a wonderful opportunity to travel to a place I probably would have never gone to, at no expense whatsoever to myself.

Once in Barcelona, we stayed at the W Barcelona Hotel. It was a beautiful hotel that sat right on the Mediterranean Sea. My room on the eleventh floor was just the right level for a fantastic view. At sunset, I witnessed the great ball of fire that seem to rest peacefully on the chest of the glistening calm sea. And, at night, the city lights beamed fancifully on the slightly restless waves.

An older co-worker, on the other hand, didn't seem quite as impressed with the accommodations. I guess what we see and how we see them all depends on one's perspective because it was simply unfathomable to me how she could not see the beauty of it all.

When I pondered perspective, my mind went back to a movie I once saw called Vantage Point. It starred some well-known Hollywood names like Forest Whitaker, Sigourney Weaver, Dennis Quaid, and William Hurt. The movie is considered a political action thriller about an attempted assassination of the President while at a summit in Spain, though only portions of the movie were filmed there. The account of what took place was given from the vantage points of the various characters. When the shots rang out and the President was down, an eye-witness and American tourist, Forest Whitaker, came forward with pictures taken with his camcorder. The evidence he submitted, he believes, has the image of the shooter.

By the time it's all said and done, they end up with eight different perspectives or vantage points, leaving the authorities to wonder which one revealed the truth.

The world is so much different than it was just twenty years ago. Today, there is so much to contend with. So many would rather just do their own thing. Depending on someone, they can see seems to be the preferred method of building trust. Everyone has an opinion about the world, how things should operate and who deserves to be in charge. There is so much division, and no person seems to agree with the other, with everybody having their own perspective.

How often do we take time to consider God's perspective? To ponder our lives from Heaven's vantage point? Looking at our world and the people in it from a flawed viewpoint can be detrimental. Our lives have been marred by wrong choices. Relationships strained by infidelity. Spirits crushed by the judgments of others, many of whom are more stained than we are. Yet, we continue to see through fogged lenses seeing the world as one blemished with more spots than a Dalmatian.

Perilous times are upon us, and the time is nigh when our Savior shall return. Will you be ready? Will you be looking down and around and miss Him? Or, will your eyes have a changed perspective that allows you to see Heaven for what it is? A place of peace and tranquility awaits those with changed vantage points. Look beyond the hills to a place where sickness and disease will be no more. A place where there will be no cause to weep and moan. No issues to send us spiraling into a deep dark hole of depression. And, the only scars in heaven won't belong to you or me. They will be in the hands of the One who is holding us right now. When we get heaven in our view and make getting there our priority, focus, and goal, our perspectives will change, and the right actions will follow. What eternal destination are you aiming for? Have you taken time to ponder where you will spend eternity? If not, now is the time to do so. God has prepared the way so let us walk therein. People of the most-high God, clean your lenses, refocus, and look up and get your eternal home in view. Heaven has spoken. Now, let the church say Amen!

My Inspiration: For victory in life, we've got to keep focused on the goal, and the goal is Heaven.

~ Lou Holtz

HEAVEN SPEAKS TO ME: With heaven in mind, how has your viewpoint changed in the past few years? How has it changed since starting these 52 weeks of devotions? In what way have you learned to prepare for your eternal home?

_____

_____

_____

_____

_____

_____

_____

_____

_____

_____

_____

_____

Scripture Reading: Revelation 21:4; John 14:1-31; 1 Corinthians 2:9; 1 Peter 1:3-5; Philippians 3:20

PRAYER: Eternal Father, I thank you for every moment you have given me to realize just how great You are. I know that for the majority of my life, I have been nearsighted and utterly consumed by the pains of this unjust world. Help me, God, to become more farsighted and filled with hope in You and the certainty of seeing you face to face in my eternal home. I welcome you into my heart Lord and ask that You help me to prepare to meet you each day by aligning my desires with Your perfect will for my life. This I ask in Your most Holy Name. Amen!

Heaven in My View

Verse 1:
With a made-up mind, with a made-up mind
I'm willing to go all the way through
Though it cost my life
I'm willing to pay the price,
I've got heaven in my view.

Verse 2:
If it means that I have to walk alone
Or that my friends, they may be few,
I'm not gonna worry about
What others may say or do,
I've got heaven in my view.

Chorus:
With a made-up mind
With a made-up mind
There's no trial that He won't take me through
And if I live right
All of my battles He will fight
I've got Heaven in my view.

With a made, a made, a made-up mind
Oh, I've got a made-up mind
Every day I can say
Hallelu, Hallelu, Hallelu, Hallelu, Hallelu
All, all of my burdens
They may weigh me down low
But, I've got Heaven in my view.

Learn to Hear God Clearly

My sheep listen to my voice; I know them, and they follow me

John 10:27

There are many ways in which God chooses to speak to us. Sometimes he speaks through people (1 Peter. 4:11) like preachers/teachers, while at other times, he may speak through our spouse or kids, friends, and maybe even our enemies. But how much greater it would be to hear him clearly for yourself? Your ability to hear God clearly is a direct result of your intimacy with Him. It's the intimacy with God that determines the outcome of our life.

When it comes to hearing God clearly, God doesn't have a problem communicating in layman's terms so that his finite children can understand. When we don't hear God, it's because we have bad posture. Growing up, my mother would get on me about slouching and not sitting up straight. She would warn me that bad posture would cause me to not be able to walk straight later in life. She urged that I would end up walking hunched over because I would have a big hump on my back. A similar effect takes place when we don't posture ourselves to hear God clearly.

I have heard many stories of how people missed God. They misspoke or misunderstood something they thought God said. In those instances, I can almost guarantee their posture was poor and off-track somewhere. Scripture declares that God's sheep knows His voice, and no other will they follow (*John 10:27*). When we position ourselves correctly in the presence of a Holy God and seek Him with our whole hearts, we will most assuredly find Him and hear from Him. For this to happen, there are six essential heart conditions that we must have:

1. **A Listening Heart.** Sitting in the presence of God and waiting after we pray shows Him that we are anticipating Him talking back to us, that we are listening, and that we want to receive whatever instructions He wants to impart to us. Having a listening prayer centers around a clear request for His guidance. When we do this, we give God's guidance, precedence, and authority over all other voices we hear in our ears telling us to do what's contrary. But, we must be sure that what we are hearing is not our voices rebelling. When our innermost thoughts try to steer us away from what we know to be true about God and the direction He is leading us in, we must submit those thoughts to God. Bringing our thought life under subjection to the will of God rids us of the interference and static of our own wayward will. Read 2 Corinthians 10:5

2. **A Heart That Places God First.** We go to God in prayer with all kinds of petitions, emotions, frustrations, complaints, hurts, and of course, all the Why questions. The demands and expectations we put on God, not that He is incapable of handling them all, are unfair and so selfish on our part. We approach only with our wants and needs, never considering what He wants from us. He is often the last stop once we've used up all other resources. We make Him last. We share our talents with him last. We give our treasures to him last. He is certainly the last one we give our time to! Once we have settled in our hearts that he is our priority above all else and make Him first in everything concerning us, we get His attention and position ourselves to hear Him speak.

3. **A Heart That's Pure and Clean.** Scripture teaches about having clean hearts. Even David prayed and asked God to "Create in me a clean heart and renew a steadfast spirit within me" (Psalms 51:10). However, to be sure we are truly hearing God, we must cleanse our hearts of all sin by repenting of any wrongdoing. John 9:31 tells us that God does not hear a sinner's prayer unless they are a worshiper and do the will of God (or give a prayer of repentance, paraphrase). Before we approach His throne, we must humble ourselves and ask for forgiveness. And, in case there may be sins we are not aware of, we should inquire of the Holy Spirit to examine our hearts, to reveal and convict us of all our sins we may need to confess. Sincere repentance clears the pathway and opens the lines of communication between heaven.

4. **A Peaceful Heart.** Making time to rest in today's society is a major challenge for most of us. With a plethora of things to do and meetings to attend, finding time to be still is like telling an inquisitive 2-year-old to stop, be still, and don't touch anything. Their curiosity won't allow them to because it's simply not in their nature to do so. There's just too much to see, touch and explore. It's unfortunate, but even when we lay down at night and our bodies are still, our minds don't slow down long or stop, even for us to rest and be at peace. Instead, they keep spinning, sometimes out of control, and we wake up feeling utterly exhausted and drained. We must find a place and space where all distractions have been removed so our minds and spirit are still and open to hearing what our Father is saying to us (Psalms 46:10).

5. **A Trusting Heart.** Being able to approach God's throne is a privilege. We are to never go before Him with our ideas of how we think things

ought to go in our lives. He is not interested in our agendas, programs, and opinions. He is only concerned about fulfilling his divine will in our lives. He is the one in control, and we must be willing to trust His sovereign plan for every part of our lives. We may never comprehend Him in His fullness until we see Him in glory. Why? Because His thoughts and ways are so much bigger and higher than ours could ever be (Isaiah 55:8-9).

6. **A Ready Heart.** Be ready to act as soon as you hear His voice. Don't make the mistake of making excuses as to why you can't or won't and why you're not qualified like Moses did (Exodus 4) and Gideon (Judges 6). When we don't move in God's timing, we not only can delay and possibly forfeit our blessings, but God is also taking note. Our lack of trust will be recorded and read when we meet Him face to face. Thousands of years later, we are still reading about Moses and Gideon, as well as so many others, because someone deemed it necessary to record each incident for the sake of history.

Upon completing this devotional, I encourage you to put these practices to the test and ask God to fix any heart conditions you may have that might prevent you from hearing Him. I am certain that having the right posture before God will get you to where you need to be. But, hey, don't just take my word for it. Read the following testimonials of women who have tried Him and found Him to be everything they need and so much more. May what you have read in this devotional and their words compel you to keep God first, repent of any sins, work to maintain a heart of peace, and learn to trust God totally, without any reservations about the outcome. Be willing and ready to go at God's command no matter what the task. Simply be ready to obey and receive.

My Inspiration: Having your spiritual radar up in constant anticipation of His presence even in the midst of the joyful chaos and regular rhythms of your everyday living is paramount in hearing God because sometimes the place and manner you find Him is the least spectacular you'd expect.

~ Priscilla Shirer

Can You Hear Me Now?

"Are you listening to me? Really listening?"

Matthew 11:15 (The Message)

Minister Debra D. Jones

A quick search in an online Bible application will yield more than 1,000 entries in the Bible that match "God said...." Armed with this information, it would be easy to confirm that God spoke throughout Biblical times. What does that say about modern times and whether God still speaks?

Let me share a personal experience with you. There was a day that I thought I heard God speak concerning a situation.

I will honestly share that I wasn't sure it was Him speaking. Quite frankly, I had considered that perhaps God didn't talk to me as much as He used to for one reason or another. Fast forward a few hours later, and I could easily validate that God did speak to me because what I heard Him say came to pass—in this instance, very quickly. My response was, "Wow, God, it was You speaking...." The next thing I heard was, "I never stopped speaking; you were not listening."

Let me confess that it stung a bit. How or why would I dare not listen when God is speaking? I realized in that instant that there were times that I was busy and distracted, and even times when I heard Him speak but didn't like what He said, so I put it off as "Oh, that's just me thinking."

My goal is more than ever to listen intently and intentionally and hear when God is speaking. To anyone that is reading this - when God speaks – please listen. It will bless your soul.

Just Do It

... *"Whatever He says to you, do it."*

John 2:5 NKJV

Elder Alice M. Baker

It was one of those rare occasions when I ran a few minutes late for church. I rushed through the doors so I could get my seat or at least in the general area. The church was packed, and the worship attendant placed me about six rows from where I usually sit. Well, I was not pleased, especially since I could see that there were seats closer to the front. Hesitantly I took my seat next to a young couple that I did not know. I set my feelings aside and shifted to praise and worship. The presence of the Lord was in the place, and I was not going to miss what He had for me. This service included honoring our pastor for his pastoral anniversary. Suddenly, something remarkable occurred during the offering period. I had already prepared my checks for my offering and love gift to my pastor. Then the Spirit of the Lord spoke to me to sow into the couple, and He was specific in the amount. I was like, "Huh?!? God, these people do not know me. What will they think or say?" He said, "Do it!" So, I am like, "God, am I hearing You?" "Yes" "Okay, do I give it to them now?" "No, wait until service is over." When it was time to give the love gift, I could see them having a discussion from my peripheral vision. The wife wrote a check, and they gave their love gift. When service was over, I embraced both, discreetly put the money in her hand, and walked away. Two weeks later, she approached me and said she had to share something with me. What she shared was that they did not have the monies to give for the love gift but wanted to give, so they gave out of their bill money. She also shared that the amount of their check was the same amount the Spirit of the Lord instructed me to give.

God used my tardiness to fulfill His plan for His glory. I love how He will confirm when He has spoken. All He wants is for us to respond in obedience. Whatever He says, just do it! Follow the prompts, and do not lean on your own understanding.

The Christmas List

By Donna Carothers

Like most of us, Christmas is my favorite time of the year. People just seem to be a little nicer, more thoughtful, and a little more considerate. I always looked forward to the holiday, and this year (December 2007), I was in full Christmas mode. I was determined to do my best-ever holiday decorations, have ALL my Christmas cards in the mail ahead of schedule, and not leave anyone I love off my shopping list! I was nearly finished with marking the last few names off my list when I discovered I needed one more day to get the job done. So, I decided to take an unplanned personal day off work to run last-minute errands before the big holiday break. My day had begun much like any other typical weekday: I crawled out of bed at 6:30 a.m., somehow pulled myself together, and grabbed a quick bite to eat before rushing out the door. However, this day, instead of work, I was on a mission to wrap up ALL my shopping and miscellaneous errands. I was going for the gold medal in holiday preparedness! I made my rounds with clockwork precision. First, the local mall for Aunt Terry's hard-to-find gift. Next, the big box store for my hubby's electronic gift, a Post-Office drop-off, and a quick stop at the grocery store to pick up some cinnamon for my sweet potato pies before finally swinging home.

Yes, I was feeling pretty accomplished about the day's events and how well I had managed my time. Christmas carols were playing on the radio, and I sang out loud the whole drive home. As I finally turned the corner to my street with my home just a few houses away... BAM, out of nowhere, it hit me like a ton of bricks! I FORGOT a gift! How could that be? I've ALWAYS been the highly efficient one in my family. Besides, I made my holiday list and checked it twice! My to-do list was done. I was just a few yards away from pulling into my driveway, feeling the sweet comforts of home and the opportunity to sneak gifts inside before my husband made it home from work. And then, in my spirit, I heard very clearly the words DO NOT GO HOME NOW. Before I knew it (really, I still don't know how it happened), I found myself driving in the opposite direction from home. I took it that I was truly supposed to get that last gift. So off I went to secure the very last gift on my list.

Two hours later, I finally pulled up in my driveway. As I made it to my doorstep with keys in hand, I knew instantly something was wrong. When I put in my key to unlock my door, I was immediately met with an eerie gust of cold wind. As my eyes found their focus across the dimly-lit hallway, it became painfully clear... our perfect holiday home had just been robbed!! All the gifts that I had brought previously for loved ones and carefully wrapped were gone. My holiday decorations and beautiful tree were all a ransacked mess. And the most private areas of our home seemed completely violated.

As I gathered the few breaths I could, I found the energy to run to my neighbor's home to find refuge and call the police to report the incident. After canvassing my neighbors, I soon learned greater details about the full aspects of the day. It turns out that the robbery took place around 4:30 pm—the very same time when I was headed home earlier in the day before I realized that I needed to get that last gift. Making a right turn onto my street would have placed me directly in the midst of the burglary (and maybe even something more terrible). But God, through his spirit, had me turn left and took me in an entirely different direction...a split-second decision that quite possibly could have saved my life!!!

Now, years later, as I remember that fateful day, I am certain that God was with me to lead, guide, and protect me from harm. I may have lost some things in the break-in, but insurance replaced all of that. The greater lesson learned is that sometimes on the roads we travel in life, we can get a little distracted and, off-course even. But if we just allow God's spirit to guide us and listen to his gentle whisper, he will always bring us to a place of peace and protection.

Hearing God Clearly

"Why spend money on what is not bread, and your labor on what does not satisfy? Listen, listen to me, and eat what is good, and you will delight in the richest of fare. Give ear and come to me; listen, that you may live. I will make an everlasting covenant with you, my faithful love promised to David."

Isaiah 55:2-3

By Sherry McDonald

It's funny how we come into our Christian walk with preconceived ideas and thoughts about who God is and how He moves and interacts with us. As a "baby saint," I thought that God would never speak to me. I had no role or position in the church and felt that I wasn't prestigious enough to be spoken to. As I matured in my relationship and understanding of God, I quickly began to learn how incorrect I was. God wants to be in a relationship with us, and He desires to commune with us.

I have found that I hear God clearly when I prepare to hear him. I focus on the state of my internal thoughts and external surroundings. First, I turn my attention to the internal chatter - What am I thinking? What am I listening to? What am I reading? What am I speaking? Too much internal, spiritually toxic noise can block us from hearing the voice of God clearly. Second, I evaluate what is going on around me. Am I moving about when God is calling me to be still? Am I setting time aside to pray or sit quietly, expecting to hear God speak? I set the atmosphere in prayer and filled the atmosphere with praise and worship from my mouth. Just as I would prepare to entertain or spend time with my close friends, God is expecting me to prepare a place for Him to come and spend time with me. It is through my intentionality of preparing to receive Him is when I hear Him speak to me ever so clearly.

Thanks for Dinner

◆◆◆◆◆◆◆◆◆

*Always giving thanks to God the Father for everything, in
the name of our Lord Jesus Christ.*

Ephesian 5:20

By Gail Smith

"Thanks for dinner, Mom," he said this morning and every morning when he greets me. "Thanks for what? I thought. That's the food you bought." But then I clearly heard the Lord in my heart say, "That's all I want from you—a little gratitude." At that moment, I felt so humbled and contrite, and my mind became overwhelmed with remorse and thoughts of how I could do better. My son and I share a home, and as he works nights and eats only when he's hungry—unlike someone else I know, but I'm learning—I try to have hot food prepared for him when he gets off from work. That's what my momma did for me, and that's what I do for him.

But back to my story. When God impressed upon me "gratitude," I ran a mental check for any time I may not have shown gratitude. I say grace before eating. I give at church. I help those I feel are less fortunate than I and do other acts of charity, so when have I not shown you gratitude, Lord? Suddenly, the simple act of eating was illuminated before me. I understood how much I take for granted. Last evening's dinner of rice, fish, and vegetables represented the labors of some workers who, unlike me, cannot work from home. Even if the rice was only from Kansas—a couple of states over from me, the hard work of planting, harvesting, sorting, packing, shipping, and all the other tasks associated with getting the rice to my local grocery store could not have been done from somebody's home desktop or laptop computer. I realized how spiritual preparing and eating food is—both of these acts are too often taken for granted. For instance, sometimes I used to stand and eat, which annoyed my mother so very much. Today I understand why that bothered her. Too busy to sit was my reason, but is that ungrateful or what?

Gratitude draws so much from a grateful heart, and our good and gracious God desires that we slow down enough to just say more than a mindless thanks with our attitude while reflecting on even the processes that bring the food to our homes for us to prepare with the strength and know-how God gave us. "Thanks for dinner, Mom."

Amazing how much like my son's voice is God's voice with the message I needed to hear for the day. "That's all I want from you—a little gratitude."

What God Has Spoken to Me

When Heaven Speaks

When Heaven Speaks

When Heaven Speaks

When Heaven Speaks

When Heaven Speaks

When Heaven Speaks

When Heaven Speaks

When Heaven Speaks

When Heaven Speaks

When Heaven Speaks

www.ingramcontent.com/pod-product-compliance
Lightning Source LLC
Chambersburg PA
CBHW032222080426
42735CB00008B/676